Thirsty
Work

Matt Skinner

Thirsty Work

Love Wine Drink Better

Photographs by Chris Terry

RUNNING PRESS
PHILADELPHIA • LONDON

© 2005 by Octopus Publishing Group Ltd, London, UK
Text copyright © Matt Skinner 2005
Photography copyright © Chris Terry 2005
All rights reserved under the Pan-American and International Copyright Conventions

Printed in China

9   8   7   6   5   4   3   2   1
Digit on the right indicates the number of this printing

Library of Congress Control Number: 2005924489

ISBN-13: 978-0-7624-2533-4
ISBN-10: 0-7624-2533-4

Commissioning Editor: Hilary Lumsden
Executive Art Editor: Yasia Williams-Leedham
Cover Design: Bill Jones
Edited for North America: Diana Von Glahn

This book may be ordered by mail from the publisher.
Please include $2.50 for postage and handling.
But try your bookstore first!

Running Press Book Publishers
125 south Twenty-second Street
Philadelphia, Pennsylvania 19103-4399

Visit us on the web!
www.runningpress.com

I HAVE LEARNT MORE ABOUT WINE FROM MATT THAN ANYONE ELSE and I think it's because he makes the whole subject so accessible. Rather than talking lots of jargon he explains in simple terms how wine works.

Matt is a modern-day ambassador for wine – he is young, vibrant, and as in love with food and wine as he is with life, skate boarding, and surfing! After meeting about five years ago we became great friends and I knew he would be the right person to help me set up Fifteen. I needed someone who could teach unemployed kids (who had never drunk wine before, let alone thought they were worthy of an opinion) about the whole world of wine. Matt's extraordinary ability to connect with people without being pretentious or patronizing is a good example of what Fifteen is all about.

He gives memorable reference points which will allow you to have an intelligent conversation with any sommelier, your local wine seller or just over dinner with your mates. He has made me think of wine as an ingredient to mix with food and not as just a drink. This has definitely made my cooking more interesting and tastier. Food and wine are like best mates who have always been destined to get together!

This book is a real turning point as far as books about wine are concerned. Matt's emphasis is on accessibility and a bit of fun. But, he'll also show you how to get good value and pleasure from your wine while at the same time encouraging you to be a bit more savvy when you're out buying your next bottle. How great is that?!

Matt, you deserve this book mate and I know you are going to make a difference.

Big Love,

THE BEST THING ABOUT WINE IS KNOWING THAT YOU'LL NEVER KNOW IT ALL.

And even though that wasn't the first piece of good advice thrown my way, it's the one bit that I'll never forget. Also worth remembering is that great wine is made everywhere – not just in your own backyard. How true that is. Great wine really is made all over our planet, and as wine-lovers, or even just drinkers with little wine experience, we owe it to ourselves and our taste-buds to try as many different wine styles from around the globe as we can possibly fit into our short and action-packed lives!

This is purely and simply a book about wine. It's not a guide. It will however, go some distance to introducing you to wine the product. And fingers crossed, it will arm you with a little more confidence, knowledge and enthusiasm no matter how much or how little you know about wine. Twenty-four hours a day, seven days a week, 365 days a year, irrespective of sex, religion or race, the wine industry brings together people from all walks of life to carry out some amazing jobs, and that in itself is a very cool thing. Shot chronologically, on the following pages you'll find profiles of a handful of these people.

Whether or not you choose to read on, remember this: with wine, there are no right or wrongs – just personal preferences. In that respect, wine is a bit like music or art. What you and I like may be two completely different things, but at the end of the day neither one of us is right – we just have different tastes. And, in a strange kind of way, that's what makes the world go round!

Happy Drinking Always,

matt

1am | Dave and Tracy the harvester team | the brains
during the harvest, logistics experts
work around the clock ensuring the grapes are picked and transported in perfect condition.

2am | Hamish the cellarhand | the muscle

cellarhands work through the night

**to keep the winery functioning like clockwork.
All year there's plenty to do in the winery.**

basics
what to know

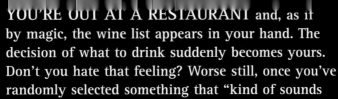

YOU'RE OUT AT A RESTAURANT and, as if by magic, the wine list appears in your hand. The decision of what to drink suddenly becomes yours. Don't you hate that feeling? Worse still, once you've randomly selected something that "kind of sounds familiar...", you may just find yourself at the mercy of a sommelier who really cares very little about what you think, and does his best to stop himself from smirking when you give your order. This sort of nightmare can be all it takes to turn you off wine for good.

You're running late for dinner with friends – friends who know their wine. You don't, so you run to your local wine shop. Surely they can help! It's fish on the menu, you want white but there are two gigantic fridges bursting with a dizzying range of bottles – where do you start? You grab the one with the most sophisticated label and head for the counter. "I just wanted to know if this would be a good choice?" "Sure," comes the unconvincing reply.

Long before these awkward, but common, scenarios there were people who really did care about what you thought – a delivery driver, a store man, a sales rep, another delivery driver, a warehouse manager, a winemaker and team, a vineyard manager and picking team, and long, long before that there was someone with a vision who cared the most. The world of wine is a truly amazing place, and, on the whole, it's full of people who care!

To avoid situations like those mentioned above, it helps to know the basics. That doesn't mean you need to know bucket loads of useless wine facts – just a few key pointers to help make Highway Nine that little bit easier to navigate. If you never learn another thing about wine, remember this: there's more to life than house wine; Chardonnay is not evil; scores out of 10, 20, even 100, aren't important; screwcaps are not an indication of cheap wine; drinking organic wine will not save you from a hangover; back labels will not tell you "how bad" the wine is; some red wines do go with fish; more alcohol doesn't mean better wine; Chablis is a place - not a grape variety, and most importantly, you generally get what you pay for.

Keeping all of this in mind, let's get down to business...

grapes

Grapes rock! Imagine a world without them... It doesn't really bear thinking about, but try if you will, and picture this.

Supermarket shelves would be choc full of all kinds of strange "it's wine Jim, but not as we know it" - type products – probably made from things like beetroot, rhubarb, milk thistle, and dandelion. Urghhh! Scary stuff.

Food wouldn't be anywhere near as exciting, nor taste as good for that matter, 'cos at the end of the day, what's food without its liquid soulmate? Millions of cellars would no longer be cellars, instead just big, soulless empty spaces under houses.

But, worst of all, the most horrible thing about a world without grapes would be that hundreds of thousands of people from all walks of life would never have the opportunity to do the amazing jobs that the wine industry allows them to do every single day.

The grape is the star ingredient in the product that we've come to know and love as wine. Kind of like the workings inside a clock, the motor in a car, the drummer in a band, the strings on a guitar, the air in your football..., you get what I mean – grapes are number one, and without them, the final product just wouldn't be wine.

Grapes are the fruit of grape vines.
A fancy species known as *Vitis vinifera* produces grapes that are specifically grown for the purpose of wine production. Wine grapes, as opposed to standard table grapes (the ones you eat on the sly at the supermarket – yeah, I've seen you!), tend to be smaller, have thicker skins, and contain pips. There are other species too – mainly the eating kind – but nearly three quarters of all the grapes produced on this planet are done so for the specific purpose of making wine.

Vitis vinifera is mum and dad to nearly a thousand different varieties. And even though – a bit like people – each variety has its own distinctive personality, there are a couple of basic characteristics that are common to all. First, a ripe grape consists of roughly 85 per cent water, 13 per cent sugar with the remaining 2 per cent being skin and pips. Sounds pretty simple, hey? Forget it, this is a complex and demanding creature in which sun, heat, water, soil, and location all play a critical role. Allow me to introduce you to the made-for-wine grape!

vitis vinifera is mum and dad to nearly a thousand different varieties

Grapes love sunshine, but not too much. It's a super fine line between too much and too little. Like other fruit, too much sun will burn the grapes; too little and they won't ripen properly. But how much sun is enough? To protect from the elements, grape vines cleverly produce a natural canopy of leaves – think of a big sombrero. Some grape varieties produce more leaves than others which, if needed, can be thinned by hand or machine to let more sun get to the fruit. But these same leaves also act as big solar panels providing the vine with its energy via photosynthesis. Take away too many leaves and the vine will lose its ability to generate the power it needs to function. Leave too many on and you run the risk of never ripening your grapes.

Grapes like it hot, but again, not too hot. In an ideal world, your "picture perfect" vineyard would be subjected to long, warm sunny days and cool breezy nights. However, as we all know, reality is rarely perfect, and in really hot climates, grapes will have a tendency to ripen too quickly giving grapes that look ripe, but aren't actually ripe to taste. This is just the same as a really hot oven burning the outside of a cake while leaving the inside uncooked.

Long, warm days ensure a slower, steadier ripening, or "even ripening", where not only will the skins, pips, and stalks all ripen together, but the grapes will also have the right sugar level. Trust me, all of this makes a big difference to the taste of the wine.

The other problem with excessive levels of temperature – hot or cold – is the threat of the vines shutting down. Vines have a natural safety switch that enables them to stop functioning in the face of extreme weather conditions. Too hot and the vines will stop photosynthesizing. Too cold and they'll head for hibernation.

a bit like us
vines need water to survive

Grapes also love to get wet, but not too wet. A bit like us, vines need water in order to survive, but given too much they'll become bloated and lazy, which results in bland-tasting fruit and lots of it. Most vineyards are naturally starved of water. This means the vines are forced to sink their roots deeper underground in an effort to search for both water and nutrients. And, hard-working vines = better grapes!

3am | Jean-Paul and Chris the pickers | the brave ones

picking grapes is a tough job

– sunburn, rain, backache, and cut fingers are what the pickers brave each vintage around the globe.

Grapes love bad soil. Chalk, clay, marl, limestone, ash, slate, loam, gravel, schist, and granite – vines thrive in all of these! Think about the veggie patch in the backyard: all dark, rich, fertile, and jammed full of good plant food like nitrogen and potassium. Now think of the opposite: exposed, nutrient-starved, all broken up and rough as you like – you're picturing grape-growing heaven! In fact, the best vineyards in the world are planted in some of the poorest, nastiest, most unforgiving soils you could ever dream of. Again, it comes back to the harder the vine has to work, the better the grapes.

Finally, grapes love to get high. I'm talking about altitude! Let me explain. We're not talking Mount Everest-like heights here, but there are a couple of big advantages for those who choose to plant their vineyards on the side of a hill and not on the flat. First, slopes provide great natural drainage, which will ensure that your vines never get too much water. Second, the poorest soils are often found up the hill where the rains wash all the nutrient-rich topsoil away, and not down below. And, lastly, slopes often get the most direct sunlight. So as well as enjoying maximum sunshine, your vines will also get cooler average temperatures as the higher you go the cooler it gets. Perfecto!

history

Now, before you think to yourself "oh great, here comes the history section – quick, flick the page", pause for a second and have a think about this. The fact that wine is such a big part of modern day culture is in no small part due to much hard work from a mass of people over many thousands of years.

Wine's journey through history has been a long and, at times, rocky road. From regular cameo appearances right the way through to the odd leading role (check out Jesus' first miracle), wine has been part of many significant events throughout time.

But the one thing that continues to amaze me is that in nearly 8,000 years of recorded wine production, the principle of how we make wine (I'm talking about the fermentation of grapes here) and the way in which we consume it has hardly changed at all. That in itself is a pretty fantastic thing.

Kicking off a little over 10,000 years ago, wine history has it all – from pharaohs and sphinxes through to Roman gladiators, monks, near total devastation, and then rebirth. The story of wine is important – you're part of it right now...

Rewind back about 10,000 years or so to ancient Mesopotamia, and we get our earliest look in on ancient vineyard management. Historians and archaeologists unearthed what they believed to be fossilized grape pips. And, it was the fact that the pips were tear shaped, not round (indicating that the vines had been pruned for harvest) that lead them to believe that this was the first real evidence of early grape cultivation.

Picture this: it's the early 1900s and yet more archaeologists are working "Indiana Jones-style" on previously unchartered Egyptian tombs. They discover a series of wall paintings that depict ancient Egyptians working in vineyards, crushing grapes, and (importantly) drinking from early wine jugs, otherwise known as amphorae.

Dated circa 6000BC this collection of artifacts found over time showed that wine was a much-loved part of ancient Egyptian culture. In fact, wine was regarded with such high social regard, that when you died – providing you were reasonably well-heeled – you were buried with a stash of great wine just in case you bumped into old pals in the afterlife. Nice touch. Let's just hope they remembered to throw in a corkscrew!

historians and archaeologists
unearthed what they believed to be fossilized grape pips

greeks, romans, and monks

Fast-forward about 5,000 years to 1,000BC and thanks to the Greeks, the wine industry was in pretty good shape. Many parts of what is now Italy, Spain, and North Africa were already under vine and wine was socially accepted. A few years later, around 50BC, the Roman Empire made some of the greatest advances the wine industry has seen to date. Organized planting, specific site selection, planting of individual varieties, barrel-making, better equipment, and, in typical Roman fashion, lots of it! Under the Romans, major plantings occurred in northern Europe and at this point, many of France's great vineyards sprang to life. Moving towards 500AD, the fall of the Roman Empire saw the beginning of the dark ages – vineyards were destroyed and little wine was consumed. Then the European monasteries came to the rescue, carefully preserved wine traditions, and brought back happier days. The next 500 years, under the watchful eye of the church, saw winemaking and grape-growing refined, with a major focus on hygiene and general vineyard practices. By the start of the 1600s, wine was back on track and expanding rapidly.

the bottle

Hit the brakes around 1650 and you may well stumble across the evolution of the glass bottle, the cork, and the corkscrew. We loved glass so much that many of the bizarre bottle shapes being produced even had names! There was the Shaft, the Onion, the Mallet, and – wait for it – the Bladder!

Today, we've simplified things to three basic shapes: Modern German, Modern Bordeaux, and Modern Burgundy, which pretty much account for all varieties from all major regions worldwide. Pretty boring, hey? Historically, bottles varied in shape for the benefit of the consumer. Early bottle shapes made specific wine styles easily recognizable, but recently it's been a bit of a free for all, and with the addition of frosted glass, colour, and odd shapes, it kind of seems that nowadays anything goes!

For the record, the construction of a bottle does have an impact on the liquid inside. For example, the trend in bottle design toward thicker, taller bottles that are darker in colour is a combination that proves really useful for ageing; the colour and thickness of the glass protect the wine from excessive light and temperature fluctuations.

early bottle shapes made specific wine styles easily recognizable

the louse

As the wine industry began its global assault, the rise of the shipping industry during the Industrial Revolution was underway, and with it came the international tourist. Not long after, the grape vine was forced to face one of its greatest challenges – phylloxera.

Most commonly spread by foot (*i.e.* the tourist), phylloxera is a root-eating louse that destroys whole vines by munching away at their foundation until they subsequently fall over and die. Not good. During the mid-1800s, phylloxera attacked and wiped out much of Europe's winemaking area before spreading to other parts of the world with a similarly devastating result. By the early 1900s, pretty much all of the wine world was gone. Only the vineyards of North America were resistant to phylloxera. A concentrated, and thankfully successful, global effort kicked off in a bid to replant the world's vineyards, this time using the American "phylloxera-resistant" rootstock.

One hundred years on and the major wine producing regions of the world have been successfully re-established, recovered, and they are now very much back in the game.

revolution

Apart from a handful of wars, prohibition, and a few close shaves with Mother Nature, the last 150 years have (touch wood!) seen the wine industry enjoy a period of relative stability and calm. Science and, in particular, Pasteur's theory of fermentation and pasteurization, has allowed winemakers to better understand and control what happens in the winery.

What this means is that, apart from the odd contaminated cork (around five to seven per cent of all corks produced are contaminated, collectively costing the industry billions of dollars each year), we can now pretty much drink technically correct wines each time we knock the top off a new bottle.

And, finally, the undeniable rise of the New World. The better part of the past 150 years has witnessed the short and seemingly glamorous rise to international stardom for much of the southern hemisphere's flourishing wine industry, and in particular Australia. Having developed a solid reputation in international markets (especially the UK) as a country producing clean, fruit-driven wines, Australia along with its New World allies (South America, South Africa, and New Zealand) have firmly proven themselves as major forces in the global wine community, putting Europe's wine-producing countries on notice.

All of which brings us to the now.

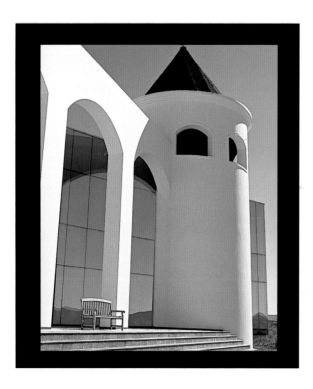

Miles and Gunter the winemakers | the creators

even winemakers
get the odd day of

The planet's next wine generation is well-travelled
and as passionate about wine as they are about life

product

While the gigantic jigsaw of wine consumers varies from thirsty student right through to conscientious collector, one thing remains more certain than ever – in the twenty-first century, wine is big business.

How we drink wine. One explanation for the switch to New World wines is the simplicity of their labels. These tend to be varietal (Chardonnay, Cabernet, Shiraz), rather than traditional regional labelling (Burgundy, Bordeaux, Hermitage) favoured by much of the Old World. To understand regional labelling, consumers need to have an extra dimension of knowledge in order to know what varieties can and can't be grown by law in that region. Tricky stuff!

The way in which we buy wine is changing, too. Supermarkets are on the way up, while corner stores are on the way out. In 2003, more than half of the wine sold in the USA was through supermarkets, while in the UK, four Goliath-like supermarkets account for around seventy per cent of all wine sales.

Who makes wine. Currently Italy sports the heavyweight title as the world's leading producer of wine by volume, surpassing France, South America, and the USA for the honours. Surprisingly however, Australia – the current darling of the wine world – shows up at around tenth position. The year 2003 saw the global wine industry punch out in excess of two billion cases – that's almost thirty billion bottles and a truckload of hangovers! At present, the global wine community is home to approximately three million people, whose roles vary far and wide from production, sales and marketing through to writers, sommeliers, and judges. Twenty-four hours a day, seven days a week, 365 days a year, the world of wine is non-stop, and in more than one sense, this really is Thirsty Work!

toolbox
what you need

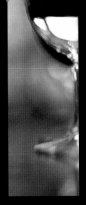

OK, SO THIS ISN'T YOUR AVERAGE TOOLBOX.
This is the Thirsty Work toolbox, and it's jammed full
of handy goodies that you already own – tools that
you may never have really known how to use. Until
now that is...

My "fab five" are attitude, ears, nose, mouth, and eyes (roughly
in that order) – there couldn't be five more important pieces of
equipment. Together, they provide the basis upon which you can
construct and develop both your tasting ability and your knowledge.

I remember Aussie wine writer Max Allen once said something like,
"approach wine in the same way as learning to ride a bike. First,
you need courage – you have to really want to do it. Hop on, and
with direction and patience, all will come together. There will be
spills on the way, but soon you won't need any help. The more
confident you become, the easier it will seem. You'll know your
equipment and then you'll wonder what all the fuss has been about".

I can't tell you how important it is to have the right attitude
around wine. This is critical. Try to approach wine with an open
mind. Don't become complacent or stuck with certain countries,
regions, varieties, or producers. Take yourself outside your comfort
zone – always try new things and never ever forget that great wine
is made everywhere and all over the planet.

Remember that your opinion is exactly that – don't try to force it
on anyone else, but at the same time, stick to it like glue. Rely
heavily on your first impressions – I reckon that they're usually
right. Try not to be overly influenced by what other people think,
but remember to keep listening to those around you – your ears are
your second most important tool! Then there's the whole language
thing to consider! This is where it all starts to get confusing. So,
along with getting your head – and tongue – around all those
strange adjectives found in the wine dictionary, learning how to
taste properly is the key ingredient to taking your next solid steps
in wine. Get the tasting part right and I guarantee you'll be well
and truly on your way. Anyway enough of the talk – ready for a
bit of sensory cross-training?

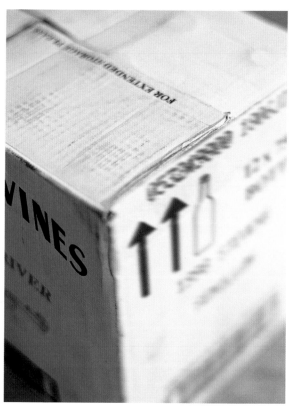

how to taste

Learning to taste wine correctly can be about as humiliating as your first time at karaoke. Less comforting still is the fact that, as a rule, wine tasting lugs around a nasty stereotype of pin-stripe suits, dodgy bow ties, and ultra-serious attitudes. Trust me, that isn't what it's like! And, besides, life's way too short for that – wine is for everybody, and learning how to taste it properly, while not essential, will help you to get the most out of every glass you put your lips to.

As I've said before, your senses are the most incredible set of tools you own, and the more actively you look, smell, taste, and listen, the quicker you'll develop your ability to identify and remember loads of different aromas and flavours. And that will mean you're actually tasting wine – rather than just guzzling it!

One final bit of advice before we get down to business. Don't forget to ask all those questions you've always been too afraid to ask, no matter how stupid you think they might be – passion, knowledge, and enthusiasm are never measured in pin-stripes or dodgy bow ties! So go on, go forth and practise, practise, practise... Oh, and it might be a good idea to remember to spit occasionally, too (more on that later)!

13

14

sight

Before we kick off, make sure that the environment is right.
Good light, preferably natural, is a must, and something
white to use as a backdrop for your glass (a tablecloth if
you're fancy or just a sheet of white paper if you're not)
will help you to determine the colour and clarity of your
chosen subject. Unfortunately, a paper cup's not going to cut
it here – a clear glass with a tapered rim is essential if you
plan to see or smell anything!

Fill your glass about a third of the way to the top (or even
better, fill it to the brim and drink the top two-thirds!) – too
much wine in your glass will stop you from being able to
swirl and smell it properly.

what colour is the wine? does the colour go right to the edge of the glass, or does it fade away?

15

16

Then take your partner by the hand – oops, sorry, flashback to those barn dancing days! – I mean take the glass by its base or the lower part of its stem, but not the bowl as the heat from your hand will increase the temperature of the wine. Tilt the glass away from you at an angle (45 degrees to be precise) and hold it against your backdrop to give you a better idea of both the depth of colour and the level of clarity.

What colour is the wine? Does the colour go right to the edge of the glass, or does it fade away? Is the wine cloudy and dull like a goldfish bowl in need of a good old clean, or does it appear clear and bright like you might imagine the Mediterranean

Sea to be? Now, as a general rule of thumb, white wines will get darker with age, while reds will tend to get lighter. You have to be careful here, though, as the appearance of some varieties can be totally misleading.

Appearance. The red variety Pinot Noir is a great example of how easily you can be tricked by appearance. Naturally pale in colour, Pinot can lead you to think that it's actually far older than it is. Add to this the fact that the best examples of Pinot Noir are often bottled unfiltered, when judged entirely on appearance, you might just get the impression that this wine is in less than average condition – until, of course, you give it a good old sniff.

Legs. You might hear people talking about this. It's a term that refers to the amount of glycerol (an indication of alcohol) in a wine. Some wines will cling to the glass when you give them a good swirl, while others will appear thinner and less viscous. The most important thing to remember is that whether or not you can see wine clinging to the side of a glass, it really doesn't have any bearing on the overall quality of the wine.

In everyday life, we tend to use our eyes more than any other sense, and it's for this reason that when we first taste wine, we tend to rely on sight way too much. Sight is the least important of your "wine senses" – use it only to give you a few clues as to what may or may not be in the glass in front of you.

20 HAVE A GOOD SNIFF

21 CAREFUL SKINNER!

22 LISTEN TO OTHERS

23 PRACTISE!

smell

Call me strange, but there are times when I actually prefer just smelling what's in my glass rather than drinking it – sounds odd doesn't it? But, in my defence, wine is a living, breathing, ever-evolving thing, and the longer it sits in your glass the broader the range of aromas you're likely to experience.

If you are even just the slightest bit unhappy about the size of your nose, you will be very pleased to know that when it comes to wine "big is better" – take it from me! Located behind the top of your nose is the olfactory nerve which is kind of like "Mission Control" for smell and taste. During the course of a lifetime, your olfactory nerve (about the same size as a small coin) will register as many as 10,000 different aromas, conveniently filing the most common for regular use. How good is that?

Smell is the most important of all your senses and your greatest asset when evaluating wine. That reminds me, I really need to look into getting my nose insured...

So, how do we do it then? OK, here we go.

33

34

35

chances are that you

A good old swirl. Start by bringing your glass up to your nose and have a good smell. What's there? Not much? Let's have another go, only this time give the glass a good old swirl before you have a smell. No doubt you'll end up covered in wine (a very Matt Skinner thing to do!), but try putting the glass on a steady surface, hold the stem kind of like you would a pencil, and move the glass in small circles as if you were repeatedly tracing around the outside of a coin. Five good quickish rotations should be enough to do the trick.

Have another smell! Bang! Big difference – like someone turned up the volume! By rotating the glass you're simply breaking the wine's surface, which in turn helps to release aroma. What do you smell now?

Listen to others. Don't worry too much if you can't think of a word to describe what you're smelling – practice makes perfect and one of the best ways to learn is to listen to people who have more tasting experience than you.

Chances are that you already know the smells, you just need the right words to associate with them, and tasting with other people will undoubtedly open up a whole suitcase full of useful trigger words to help you put a "name to a face", so to speak.

taste

In case you didn't know, your mouth and nose are joined! You must have seen the old "spaghetti up the nose and out the mouth" trick? Sorry for the scary visuals, but it's pretty important to note that even though the two are indeed connected, your mouth isn't nearly as good at identifying the same number of flavours as your nose.

At the end of the day, what you taste is merely just a simplified version of what you smell, but, that said, your mouth – unlike your nose – is a great tool for detecting texture.

Texture is "what you feel", like hot and cold, as opposed to "what you taste", and, in the case of wine, that means body, acid, tannin, and alcohol. Let me explain.

Body. And no, I'm not talking about Kylie here guys! Body is a term used to describe the weight of a wine, or how it feels in your mouth.

Is it light and delicate like a mouthful of fresh water from a stream, or does it feel much heavier – like milk?

already know the smells, you just need the right words

36 SWISH IT AROUND   37 DON'T DRIBBLE!   38 TASTE WHAT?

36

37

38

5am | Adrian the warehouse manager | the gatekeeper

while most of us are still sleeping,

warehouse managers are hard at it picking, sorting, checking, packing, and delivering truckloads of wine all over the globe.

polyphenols help to lower cholesterol
and blood pressure

Acid is a natural preservative that is found in all wine. It's what makes green Granny Smith apples taste tart. It is essential in wine, as it acts like a skeleton around which the fruit is built. Without acid, your wine would taste limp and out of balance. You register acid on the sides of your tongue, where it leaves a slight tingling sensation, which most people describe as crisp.

Tannin is a type of acid that comes from grape skins, grape pips, and wood. You can't smell or taste tannin, but it's that really dry feeling that you get after a big gulp of red wine. Apart from giving wine structure, tannin is an incredibly useful tool for cutting through things like fat and the texture of red meat. And if you're still not sure what tannin feels like, then you could always try sucking on a teabag? Perhaps that might be a touch excessive... On a more serious note, tannin is a natural antioxidant and contains polyphenols. Polyphenols help to lower both cholesterol and blood pressure, stimulate the immune system and, we think, protect your body against "The Big C".

Alcohol is the result of fermentation, but more about that later. A wine with a lot of alcohol will feel slightly hot at the back of your mouth. However, a well-made wine should always have enough fruit concentration to balance out alcohol, so, in fact, you should never really be able to notice that "hot" character.

How do we pull all these characteristics together in order to "taste"?

let's get tasting...

You'll see people pull some pretty funny faces when they taste wine, but I promise it's for a good reason. In order to taste wine correctly, you take a small amount into your mouth and swish it around for a few seconds – a bit like you'd do with mouthwash. The reason for this is to completely coat the inside of your mouth so that it detects things in different places.

Suck. This next bit can be a little tricky if, like me, you're inclined to dribble! Here come those funny faces! With the wine in your mouth, try sucking a little air through your lips, holding it there for a few seconds. To get this right, think about how you whistle – suck air in rather than blow it out. This process will allow air to get into the wine, better illustrating its flavours.

Swish it around your mouth. Now would be the perfect time to spit (if, of course, that's what you're planning to do!). Spit out around three-quarters of what you have in your mouth, and then swallow the rest. Trust me, you'll be thanking me if you've got more than a handful of wines to taste!

Swallow. As you swallow the wine, think about what's happening in your mouth. Where does the flavour of the wine hit your tongue? Does it taste tart? Does the wine dry out your mouth? How many seconds after you swallow can you still taste the wine? I normally taste a wine two or three times before I get busy drinking it – first to consider the flavour, second to measure its intensity, and, finally, to get an overall idea of tannin (only if it's a red wine), acid, body, length of flavour, and the general balance of the wine.

Balance is really important. Think about balance like a set of scales. With wine, you have fruit on one side, and alcohol, acid, tannin, and oak on the other. Your goal is to make the scales level, with no one thing dominating.

Wine is the sum of each of these parts – a bit like the members of a band, each one playing a vital role. And it's how they all work together that will determine if we're looking at a Top 10 hit or just another track destined for the karaoke scrap heap!

language

The scene is a room of first-time tasters – dead silent. They're contemplating the glass of ultra-pale white wine in front of them. Wine swishes high around the sides of glasses, while noses repeatedly dive in and out looking for adjectives to describe what they are smelling.

The level of concentration is evident. Early calls of "passion-fruit" and "gooseberry" from the outspoken pair down the front are good, while the words "grassy" and "herbaceous" from someone at the back are even better. But it's the young kid in the second row who, full of confidence, decides to break the silence. "I think it smells like cat's piss and sweaty armpits." The room erupts with laughter. The tutor cracks a smile. "Spot on, you're absolutely right", he replies. The young kid (yes, that was me!) has a grin that stretches from ear to ear.

science fiction

When I was getting into wine a little over ten years ago, I couldn't tell a raisin from a prune. I knew enough to know what I liked, but that was about it. Tasting aside, I found that reading proved to be the safest way to learn about wine without having to ask lots of, what I thought, were really "silly questions" – especially in front of the people I worked with!

I was like a man possessed. I bought wine magazines. I tore wine columns out of mum's Sunday newspapers. I bought wine guides off the counters of wine shops. And for some strange reason, I got hold of every second-hand and out-of-date wine book that I could dig up! Never having been a big reader, I read and I read and I read.

Bizarrely, the language of wine baffled me more than wine itself (the product). Why did such a straightforward subject attract such complicated words? I couldn't understand it.

From botrytis and Brettanomyces to carbonic maceration and clones, I remember thinking to myself that wine-lovers might actually be the largest group of underground science fiction geeks on the planet!

And then not long after I began my first serious wine job, I remember a company tasting, where someone described a wine as having "high acid"!

High acid. What on earth were they talking about? Did the wine contain acid? Did I have to drink it? Would I die if I did? Would I lose my job if I didn't? Panic stations! Thankfully, soon after, I stumbled across a couple of "new school" wine writers who broke down all the flowery adjectives and spoke to me like the true dummy that I was! What a revelation! Suddenly a lot of things began to make sense. I could see the value in what I'd been drinking, and now I was up and running.

Exotic. Wine is like an exotic foreign country that you really want to explore. Like most exotic countries, it comes complete with its own language, and unless you know more than just the token handful of lines to get you by, getting maximum enjoyment out of that country is going to be a hard assignment.

the language of wine baffled me more than wine itself

mass confusion

The language of wine can be seriously frustrating for those who are new to it. "Blowsy, firm, fat, easy, fleshy, punchy, rich, and fresh" – ding dong! The fact that many of these words are already familiar to most of us makes things a little simpler, but, in some ways, this can also make it easier to run into trouble!

Wine terms. Take the word "short", for example. Short means small or not tall, right? Wrong. In wine terms, the word "short" refers to a wine where the flavour finishes very quickly in your mouth. The word "flabby" is another one. What does it mean to you? Is it a hamburger-enriched Elvis in a white jumpsuit, or is it a wine that lacks balance and structure due to low acidity? In the wine world, it's definitely the latter! There are other good ones, too. From experience I've found that most people describe acidity as either "sharp" or "tangy", while "fruity" is usually mistaken for "sweet".

Know what you like. How does something so normal end up being intellectualized to the point of mass confusion? Wine is for everybody, and so long as you know enough to know what you like, what else matters? Trust me, pay very little attention to the language of wine and most importantly, never let it put you off.

PRINCE
WINE
STORE

6am | Ntsiki the graduate winemaker | the graduate

making her first wine this year,

Ntsiki can hardly wait! She knew zero about grapes before
applying for a winemaking course at Stellenbosch University.

fruit
red and white

THINK OF GRAPES LIKE YOU WOULD PEOPLE
– hundreds of different varieties, each one with its own personality. Some are delicate and pretty, others full-bodied and intense.

The emergence of new varieties occurs in much the same way a family tree develops and splinters over time. Vine cuttings are transported from one place to another, where, subjected to a different set of climatic conditions, different soils, even different kinds of diseases, they'll be forced to mutate and change, ultimately creating a brand new variety.

All varieties of grapes, red and white – just like people – can be traced back to the same point of origin, or in this case, species of vine, otherwise known as *Vitis vinifera*.

Featured in this section are my top varieties, including profiles of the most interesting red and white grapes produced on the planet. Reading alphabetically, we move through the classics onto the lesser known, and I use icons (*see* below) to indicate the styles – from light, delicate wines to richer options, and finally to the business end – the heavyweights!

Use this section as a reference tool and hopefully, by following the icon of a variety you already know, it will encourage you to try something new. For example, if you know you like Chardonnay but have never tried Grüner Veltliner, what are you waiting for?! After all, there's so much more to life than just "a glass of house white"...

Key to the icons used to indicate the style of wine:

↑ Like 'em light

↻ Not too heavy, not too light – just right

↓ Definitely not for the faint-hearted

white grapes

The question I seem to get asked most is "which do you prefer, red or white?" My standard answer, which is the truth, is that I don't really have a favourite, but having given it a bit of thought, I reckon that on a day-to-day basis I probably drink more white than I do red. In this chapter, we take a good look at my top white varieties – the movers and shakers of the white wine world. Also, I've included a rundown on a handful of lesser-known, but no less important, white varieties that you're bound to be hearing more about in the not too distant future.

chardonnay

shar-don-ay

Love or loathe it, Chardonnay is king of the white grapes and has been called many things, including "the Coca-Cola of the wine world", but when it's all said and done, you just can't deny this variety its place in wine's Hall of Fame. After all, Chardonnay is not the most feverishly consumed white grape variety for nothing!

style | I love Chardonnay. In fact, I go mad for it. And while I'm the first to admit that this grape variety can, at times, be about as interesting as watching paint dry, it's the really great examples – wines that have a dizzying range of smells and flavours – that easily rank as some of the most exciting wines in the world. The very best examples hail from Burgundy in France, where handcrafted wines rely more on texture, finesse, structure, and ageability rather than the simple "drink now" fruit flavours that you might find from other parts of the world. Chardonnay vines will sink their roots just about anywhere, and as a result, this variety varies greatly in aroma and taste depending on where it's grown. This is where the trouble with Chardonnay starts...

taste | Chardonnay comes in all different shapes and sizes. In the warmth of the southern hemisphere, aromas range from soft, stone fruit like peaches and pears through to "full throttle" ripe, tropical fruit like banana, pineapple, guava, and mango. In the northern hemisphere, flavours range from the delicate, citrusy, and slightly honeyed wines of France's Chablis district, right the way through to insanely concentrated and layered wines of the Côte de Beaune which come packing smells of super citrus, sweet spice, grilled nuts, and pork fat.

f.y.i | A few fancy moves in the winery will also determine the end result for the winemaker's signature Chardonnay. Full malolactic fermentation, barrel fermentation, and a little lees stirring (don't worry, we'll get to all of that later, *see* p.170), and "shazam", the result can be the kind of wine that most people now love to hate. It's a shame really, because there are very few Chardonnays around now that are that full on. Otherwise, things can be a little more subdued with a "less is more" approach. This usually results in the kind of wines that I, and hordes of other Chardonnay fans, absolutely love drinking.

chenin blanc

shen-an-blonk

Handier than a Swiss Army knife, the globetrotting Chenin Blanc's high natural acidity and tendency to flirt with botrytis (a type of mould that attacks and sucks water out of grapes!) lends itself equally well to the production of a variety of styles: sweet, dry, and fizzy.

style | Chenin's real stomping ground is the Loire Valley in France, where it appears as tooth-crackingly racy, dry whites; luscious, syrupy, sweet wines; and ultra-dry, super frothy fizz which make for some of the best pre-dinner drinks in the world. Outside of France, Chenin Blanc dominates the vineyards of South Africa, where, up until only a few years back, it accounted for a whopping quarter of all wine grown and produced.

taste | For all its glowing attributes, Chenin Blanc has, for some reason, taken a back seat behind its flashier cousin, Sauvignon Blanc. Possessing similar characteristics, you can expect to be bombarded with aromas of green apples, gooseberry, and fresh herbs.

f.y.i | Unlike Sauvignon Blanc which tastes best in its youth, Chenin Blanc shines in its twilight years (around ten to fifteen years), and makes for a model senior citizen – still showing all that apple and pear character, but a really attractive honeyed richness, too. It's worth seeking this variety out.

gewurztraminer

a.k.a. traminer | clevner

ger-vertz-tramina

Like an oversized drag queen with too much make-up, way too much perfume, mega high heels, and very little shame, this variety is the flamboyantly camp member of the white grape family! But, sadly, it also doubles as one of the uncoolest grape varieties in the world. In fact, it's fair to say that if Gewurztraminer were an outfit it'd be socks, sandals, and a camel brown safari suit. Try pronouncing it – apart from being much harder to say than Chardonnay, it even sounds a bit naff. And that's the problem.

style | In reality, "Gewurtz" is one of the superstar varieties of Alsace, a tiny little region located in France's northeastern corner. In recent years, countries such as Australia, New Zealand, and Chile have really stepped up to the plate and are doing fine things with this grape.

taste | As far as aromas and flavours go, Gewurtz has to go down as one of the more exotic white grape varieties around. The best examples ooze lychee, rose, orange blossom, cinnamon, ginger, flowers, and spice. Sounds pretty good, doesn't it? Typically, they'll be rich and weighty in the mouth (due to low natural acidity), and have a great length of flavour.

f.y.i | While Gewurtz doesn't share the same flexibility as some of its fellow white friends, it does make for an all-time match with a number of specific food styles, namely anything mildly spicy, tangy, or sweet. So who cares if you can't say it properly, next time you grab a Chinese take-out, exercise your "open wine mind", and grab a bottle of Gewurtz – you and your taste-buds will thank me for it!

◔ muscat

a.k.a. muscat blanc à petit grains, lunel, de Frontignan, d'Alsace, Canelli, ottonel | muskateller | moscato | moscadello | moscatel | tamîîoasa

Some of my earliest and favourite memories are of family road trips around the wineries of northeast Victoria in Australia. I can still vividly remember the smells of the vineyards, but it's the smell of those sweet, dried raisins – the same grapes that are used for the production of Muscat – that I've never forgotten.

style | Muscat comes in many forms (*see* above), and the range of wine styles that can be made from them is, in a word, exhausting – the light and fizzy Mosacto d'Asti of northwest Italy, the sweet and spirity Muscat Beaumes-de-Venise from France's Rhône Valley, the heady and aromatic wines from Malaga in Spain, the treacle-like Moscatel di Jerez and finally, the unique and ancient fortified Muscats of northeast Victoria, Australia.

taste | With so many different expressions, pinning down a varietal character is tough. Smells can range from pears, apples, and flowers in the lighter wines, right through to roses, coffee, and chocolate in the big monsters. In nearly all but a few cases, examples will display pure, aromatic, and, not surprisingly, grape smells. Magic!

f.y.i | If you want to check out one of the world's simplest (and best) food and wine combinations, then grab a bottle of Moscato d'Asti from northwest Italy, and serve it alongside a bowl of the freshest fruit you can find. So very good!

pinot grigio / pinot gris

a.k.a. grauburgunder | ruländer | malvoisie

pee-no gree jee-o / gree

Imagine a set of identical twins separated at birth and raised in different countries. Genetically identical, but, with a different country, comes a different language and a different style. This is the infamous Pinot Grigio and its pal, Pinot Gris.

style | Technically speaking, these guys are the same. The key difference comes down to a question of style. The most concentrated plantings of Pinot Grigio can be found in the cool of Italy's northeast, while Pinot Gris is never more at home than in the French region of Alsace. Elsewhere around the globe, New Zealand has had great success, especially with Gris, as has both the USA and, on a smaller scale, Australia.

taste | Pinot Grigio, by tradition, is the Italian expression – light, delicate, and fresh. It's usually put together in stainless-steel tanks and best drunk young while it's still really zippy and vibrant. Pinot Gris, on the other hand, is the French expression (sometimes with Tokay before its name) – fatter and richer, with more weight and intensity, often from time spent in wood.

f.y.i | While Pinot Grigio can take care of lighter, more aromatic dishes in the way of salads, fish, and seafood such as prawns and oysters, the fatter, weightier Pinot Gris – especially with a hint of sweetness there – is a killer alongside a fresh piece of pan-fried foie gras. Better examples of Pinot Gris can be stashed away with confidence for a good few years.

imagine a set of identical twins
separated at birth and raised in different countries

7am | "Gardener" the viticulturist | the gardener

looking after the
best kind of plants,

Gardener (Wayne Morrow) is a full-time viticulturist
who travels all over New Zealand looking after grape vines.

8am | Ray the driver | the wheels

with 300,000 boxes of wine in the warehouse,

Ray zips around on his fork-lift with the precision of a fighter pilot.

↻ riesling

reez-ling

For many years Riesling has been like the "Kenny G" of white grape varieties – technically brilliant, but oh so lacking in credibility. Add to this a couple of good old-fashioned wine scandals in the 1970s, not forgetting that most people think of this variety as sickly sweet, and many consumers will give Riesling the big thumbs down. However, for some time now, Riesling has been making a comeback, and apart from being awesome value for money, it is also incredibly food-friendly – particularly with Asian flavours and, of course, seafood.

style | While the spiritual home of this variety is Germany, you'll also find world-class examples from Austria, France, the USA, New Zealand, and Australia. At first, you might find some examples are a little tart – this is acid, and is essential if you plan to keep your bottles for more than a few years. And remember the Rieslings I'm talking about are bone dry rather than sweet.

taste | The best examples will have beautiful, pure, citrus fruit aromas, alongside those of fresh-cut flowers and spice, while in the mouth you'll find flavours of lemons, limes, and minerals. And while bone dry examples of Riesling are currently all the rage, there's still, thankfully, a handful of examples left in Europe made with a bit of sweetness on board – you just need to get past the labels (*see* p.144)!

f.y.i | As a final tip, Riesling, as the under-valued renaissance kid, currently represents some of this planet's great bargain wine buys. Better still, it's worth noting that this variety has amazing ageing potential, with some of the best wines easily outliving us! Go on, throw a few under the bed for a rainy day!

sauvignon blanc

a.k.a. blanc fumé

sov-in-yon blonk

Sauvignon Blanc splits opinion like no other grape I know. It's no wonder, really, considering that this variety comes complete with adjectives for describing its aromas such as sweaty armpits, cat's piss (yep, really!), tinned asparagus, and fresh-cut grass.

style | Together with Sémillon, Sauvignon Blanc plays a major role in the production of the sweet wines of Sauternes in Bordeaux. Elsewhere in France, Sauvignon Blanc is the star of the crisp, minerally wines made in Pouilly-Fumé and Sancerre in the Loire. In the New World, this variety has tasted success in South Africa and Chile, but nowhere quite as much as in New Zealand's Marlborough region – the undeniable new home of this variety.

taste | Classic Sauvignon Blanc is incredibly pale in colour and unmistakably pungent on the nose. Passion-fruit, asparagus, gooseberry, elderflower, basil, mint, and fresh-cut grass – the list goes on! Typically these are wines that are painfully (in a good way!) crisp, clean, and very refreshing, with plenty of zip and often racy acidity.

f.y.i | Sauvignon Blanc is uncomplicated, and in the absence of any David Copperfield-like tricks, the key to this variety's success with food lies in the simplicity of the ingredients you choose. While seafood, and especially shellfish, might be an obvious choice, check out goat's cheese, ricotta, and all those amazingly fresh, spring flavours, such as fresh peas, broad beans, zucchini, basil, mint, and lemon. At their best, they'll provide some mind-blowingly simple yet truly great matches for your Sauvignon Blanc.

⟳ sémillon

semee-on

At first glance, you could be forgiven
for thinking of Sémillon as being a little
like elevator music – one-dimensional and
a bit simple. But, like anything, look beyond
the exterior and you'll find the beauty
within and the magic that is Sémillon!

style | Falling head first into
the medium to full-bodied white
camp, Sémillon is native to
France's Bordeaux region. But,
it's down under in Oz, and more
specifically New South Wales'
Hunter Valley district where
Semillon (no é in Oz) has had
the greatest amount of success,
producing beautifully crafted
and insanely long-lived wines.
Elsewhere, there are scattered
plantings of Sémillon in
South Africa, Eastern Europe,
Asia, and Greece.

taste | In its youth, great
examples of Sémillon are
characteristically creamy, soft,
and bursting with pear, white
peach, and other ripe summer
fruit. Don't get me wrong, it
is great to drink young, but
be patient – stash a couple
of bottles away for a few years
down the track, and that's when
you should see some of that
magic. In older examples of
Sémillon, expect to smell intense
citrus fruit, even marmalade,
alongside aromas of toast,
honey, nuts, and sweet spice.
Now that's my kind of breakfast!

f.y.i | It's slightly surprising
that the Hunter Valley is one
of the best producing areas
of this grape, as it is an
unforgiving place where fire,
cyclones, drought, and intense
temperature fluctuations all
point toward a "big fat no" for
grape-growing, but when it all
comes together for the Hunter's
winemaking community, the
results are incredible. Hunt them
down and try.

⏷ viognier

vee-on-yeah

Not a grape variety for the faint-hearted, with a weight and feel similar to that of Chardonnay, not to mention more grunt than a monster truck. The best examples of Viognier tend to come with a trademark mega-high alcohol content –15 degrees is pretty much normal!

style | Native to the near vertical slopes of Condrieu in France's northern Rhône Valley, Viognier has recently shown heaps of promise south of the equator – especially in Australia and South Africa.

taste | Different to the tropical smells of Chardonnay, Viognier overflows with intoxicating smells of apricots, orange rind, and fresh flowers. In the mouth, it's weighty and rich, and, in some cases, even oily. It has a great length of flavour that's balanced beautifully by a low-level of natural acidity.

f.y.i | While finding suitable food matches for Viognier might prove even more difficult than passing my Jenga record of thirty-three layers, low natural acidity combined with overtly flamboyant flavours lend themselves perfectly to spicy Asian food – particularly Thai and South Indian.

cortese

cor-tay-zee

style | Cortese comes from northwest Italy and is a local variety that regularly pops up under the guise of Gavi (from the village of the same name). Great examples of Gavi are clean and dry with an almost neutral character.

taste | Expect to smell pears, limes, almonds, talcum powder, and really fresh flowers, while in the mouth it's clean, dry, zippy, and delicate with trademark fresh acidity.

f.y.i | Its simplicity makes it the perfect match for a really broad range of food styles, especially freshly shucked oysters. Hmmm, fresh flowers and oysters – now all I need is my Barry White CD, a few candles... Where's my wife?

garganega

gar-gan-ai-ga

style | Superstar producers are thin on the ground in Italy's Soave (*swar-vay*) region where Garganega plays the leading role, alongside Trebbiano and smaller plantings of Chardonnay. Sadly, over the years Soave has forged its reputation on oversized bottles of wine that look like water and taste of little more. Although perception is changing slowly, Soave's new generation of winemakers has set out in an unrelenting pursuit of quality, and is starting to produce some of the greatest (and most consistently high-quality) white wines anywhere in Italy.

taste | Traditionally, it has subtle smells of pear, apple, and honeysuckle. Garganega also benefits from a little bit of extra hang time on the vine, and even has a smidge of oak influence.

f.y.i | As a matter of interest, Garganega can also be made into some really amazing sweet wines that are hard to find, but well worth the hunt.

grüner veltliner

grew-ner velt-lee-ner

style | If you haven't heard of Grüner Veltliner, where have you been?! The past couple of years have seen Austria rocket into "white wine legend" territory – mainly for producing more than their fair share of stunning Rieslings and the uber-cool variety of the moment, Grüner Veltliner.

taste | Often likened to Chardonnay for its weight and intensity, it's Grüner's aromatics that really get me going. Different to Chardonnay, Grüner is spicier with smells of miso paste, ginger, and wet wool, while in your mouth you'll find Grüner to be full and rich, without the influence of wood.

f.y.i | Like Chardonnay, this variety can stand up to some pretty big flavours. Salmon, tuna, chicken, and pork are all good choices.

marsanne

style | One of the first white wines I ever tried was made from Marsanne, and I loved it! Clean, fresh, fruity, not too heavy, not too light – just right! While Marsanne plays very much second fiddle to Viognier in France's northern Rhône Valley, it dominates many of the white wine blends of the southern Rhône. Outside of France, you might see Marsanne pop up in parts of Australia.

taste | Expect ripe, peachy fruit flavours, fresh acidity, and barely a sniff of oak (as it doesn't cope with wood all that well). With a bit of age, Marsanne takes on an amazing honeyed character. The palate, too, becomes slightly oilier and has more weight and richness.

f.y.i | Marsanne is great with a broad range of food styles, especially fish. And while it's perfectly suited to lighter styles of fish, Marsanne also provides some great matches with fuller flavoured, even smoked, members of the fish family.

pedro ximénez
a.k.a. px

pedro him-en-eth

style | Jerez, in Spain's south, is a full-throttle cocktail of flamenco, bullfighting, dressage, tapas, kite surfing, and, of course, sherry. Now, when I say sherry, you can forget nan's drinks tray – sherry is back and it's really, really, really good! Although PX technically falls into the white grape family, this "sun-loving" variety produces insanely sweet, thick, and syrupy wines occasionally referred to as "black sherry".

taste | Great examples of PX are almost black in colour, incredibly viscous, and extra sweet with intense smells of raisin and spice.

f.y.i | The best way to drink PX is after dinner, drizzled all over great vanilla ice-cream, or by the glass with a slice or three of nan's fruit cake, God bless her!

pinot blanc
a.k.a. klevner | weissburgunder

pee-no blonk

style | Talk about keeping it in the family. Pinot Blanc is the distant love child of Pinot Gris, which just so happens to be a relative of Pinot Noir! If Pinot Blanc were a cricketer, it would be a great all-rounder. It is one of those grape varieties that's dependable, reliable, and delicious, but rarely, if ever, is it the number one choice. Planted widely in many parts of Europe and especially in Alsace, there are also smatterings throughout Germany, Italy, and North America.

taste | Pinot Blanc tends to be pretty neutral in both aroma and flavour. Pears, apples, minerals, and a touch of honey, even a slight chalkiness, is what to expect.

f.y.i | What I really love about Pinot Blanc is that it's light, delicate, and scarily easy to drink. It's the ultimate good-value summertime white, so go and buy some now!

sherry is back and it's really, really, really good!

9am | Becks the laboratory technician | the scientist

the winery lab is quality control

– responsible for testing pretty much everything to do with a wine before it's released, ready to drink.

⟲ roussanne

roos-ann

style | Ronnie and Reggie Kray, the Cheeky girls, The Olson sisters, Mark and Steve Waugh – all notable twins in their own right, and in much the same way the Kray brothers ran the show in London's East End during the 1960s, Marsanne and Roussanne are the whites that rule the roost in the vineyards of France's southern Rhône Valley. Like their Rhône cousin, Viognier, they show subtle aromatics and textures. Outside of France, Roussanne also pops up in Italy, the USA and Australia.

taste | Expect full-bodied wines full of white chocolate and stone fruit (think apricots and peaches), spice, and richness.

f.y.i | Roussanne likes to spend a fair bit of time hanging around on the vine, so you might notice that some examples come with a decent dose of alcohol, too!

⟳ verdelho

ver-del-o

style | Great examples of this grape come from Australia and Spain, where it can be both dry or sweet, and on the island of Madeira, where it pops up as one of the major blending grapes for white fortified wines. If you like Sauvignon Blanc, chances are you're going to love Verdelho, too. No matter how many times I taste Verdelho, my tasting notes always seem to read as though it is Sauvignon Blanc...

taste | This wine is a super pale colour. It smells of passion-fruit, lemon, and fresh-cut grass, while in the mouth there's plenty of ripe citrusy fruit, and a clean, crisp, and spankingly dry finish.

f.y.i | Be careful not to get Verdelho confused with the Spanish white grape, Verdejo. The two sound, look, and even taste pretty similar, but they're definitely not related!

⟲ verdicchio

ver-dik-ee-o

style | I love Verdicchio, but before you go running off to the corner store to grab yourself a couple of bottles, wait – you're going to struggle finding one. Verdicchio is grown and produced in Italy's Marche region (central Italy's eastern boarder). The problem with availability comes down to volume, as most are made by small family growers, with simply not enough to go around. That said, great Verdicchio is well worth finding should you be lucky enough to get your hands on some!

taste | These are big rich whites that are not much to smell, but super lemony in flavour with great spice and richness. Because of its weight, Verdicchio tends to handle wood pretty well, too.

f.y.i | It is a brilliant partner to many things from the sea, and a range of white meats.

if you like Sauvignon Blanc,
chances are you're going to love Verdelho, too

red grapes

From light and delicate all the way through to full-bodied, chunky, and tannic, red grape varieties are as diverse in style as they are numerous. The following pages bring to light my (remember, my) major red varieties, their key characteristics, places of origin and even the odd bit of useful "dinner party" trivia just for good measure! Some of the varieties mentioned have established and well-earned reputations that see them repeatedly popping up in all corners of the globe, while others – somewhat more obscure – are destined to be the superstars of tomorrow.

cabernet sauvignon

a.k.a. petite vidure

kab-er-nay sov-in-yon

If Chardonnay is king of white grapes, then surely Cabernet Sauvignon is ruler of the reds. The best examples of Cabernet have it all – displaying power, finesse, elegance, the ability to age, and, most importantly, universal appeal. Perhaps the most well-travelled of any of the red grapes, Cabernet has proven its worth in all winemaking corners around the world. However, as a late-ripening variety, Cabernet definitely has a thing for warmer climates where it can really strut its stuff.

style | A native of France's Bordeaux region, Cabernet Sauvignon is now well and truly established in just about every grape-growing country on earth. Particularly good examples have come from Italy, Spain, Chile, Argentina, South Africa, Australia, and California.

taste | Often dubbed the "doughnut variety" because of the way it leaves a great big hole in the middle of your palate, Cabernet Sauvignon can be blended with Merlot to fill out the wine in your mouth. As a universally produced variety, the range of flavours and aromas for Cabernet Sauvignon varies greatly. However, benchmark examples should exhibit smells of blackcurrant, dark-cherry, and plummy fruit, alongside cedar, mint, leather, and eucalyptus. Because of its thick skins and high natural acidity, the best examples are some of the longest-lived red wines to be found.

f.y.i | As a definite "full-bodied" red, Cabernet is similarly best-suited to big flavours. Meat is the match, particularly beef, where intensity of flavour will stand up to that of the wine, while Cabernet's dry, grippy tannins work to cut through the texture of the meat.

↻ grenache

gren-ash

Grenache has been around for donkey's years. Grown widely in Spain, France, and Australia, Grenache is not only the great workhorse of red grape varieties, but also a bonafide stand-alone performer in its own right. As one of the most widely planted red grape on the planet, you have to be careful not to let Grenache crop too high or it will produce vast amounts of bland wine. Recent times have seen this variety swing back into the limelight. Fruit from old vines (we're talking really ancient vines) makes some of the best examples – delicious wines that come complete with masses of depth.

style | Grenache produces weighty, concentrated, fully-fledged reds – especially out of France's southern Rhône Valley. The top examples sit comfortably alongside some of the greatest wines in the world. The "big G" is also the preferred grape variety for many styles of rosé wine, where low tannin, poor colour, zippy acidity, and even a decent whack of alcohol, are the go. It's everything you might want from a great Sunday morning Yum Cha wine (rosé, not Grenache!).

taste | Characteristically, Grenache is loaded with bright raspberry and plum fruit, supported well by trademark smells of freshly ground pepper and Asian spices, gentle acidity, and firm but low-level tannin.

f.y.i | As a rule, anything a little bit gamey or likewise, with a bit of spice is well worth a look alongside good examples of Grenache.

⚓ malbec

a.k.a. cot | auxerrois

Argentina's Andes mountains are not only home to some of the greatest snowboarding to be had, but here you'll find some of the highest-altitude vineyards planted anywhere on the planet. Perched just under 914 metres (3,000 feet) above sea level, the vineyards enjoy optimal exposure to the sun and a unique microclimate, ensuring that Malbec has a long and steady ripening. This means maximum ripeness and maximum acidity.

style | It hasn't always been smooth sailing for Malbec. For many years, internationally, if it wasn't viewed as "just another blending component", then it was being ripped out of the ground. Then along came Argentina, and with some of the oldest plantings of this grape to be found, Argentina's Malbecs are the benchmark rather than the poor second cousin. Also found in Bordeaux, Chile and pockets of Australia, Malbec is a variety that loves the sun. If you want colour, you got it! In fact, think black.

taste | These are big wines, and the best examples are soft and filled with ultra-ripe fruit, showing plenty of plums, spice, and great intensity.

f.y.i | And, as big wines, they require food with big flavours. Head for the meat department and don't be shy with spice or sweetness, as these are wines that will handle them comfortably. Olé!

if you want colour, you got it!
In fact, think black

10am | Paul and Josh the sommeliers | the help

here to help you drink better wine

the new breed of sommelier is friendly, down-to-earth, and very well-informed.

⌒ merlot

mer-low

I remember reading about Merlot and salivating over words such as "sweet, juicy, ripe, and soft", but when I finally tasted Merlot for the first time, it was thin, acidic, and smelled like tomato leaves. Had I been ripped off? No, it's just that Merlot kind of straddles the fence between lightweight and something a bit bigger – it all just hinges on where it's grown.

style | For many years, Merlot has very much played second fiddle to big brother Cabernet Sauvignon, and has often been sidelined as a great wine for blending, especially with Cabernet to add a bit more weight and intensity. Merlot is the most widely planted red grape variety in Bordeaux. And, in recent times, UK, Californian, and Australian wine-drinkers have had a love affair with this variety.

taste | Well-made Merlot is like a big, old, comfy armchair, and, at best, is packed with ripe, mouth-filling fruit and very little tannin. New World examples tend to be plump and choc full of full-on, round plummy fruit, with low natural tannin. Top styles from north of the equator tend to be drier, leaner, and less in your face.

f.y.i | Merlot's appeal lies in the fact that it's an incredibly "gluggable" variety. It's extremely drinkable and it's easy to get through multiple bottles (should you want to!).

↻ nebbiolo

a.k.a. spanna | chiavennasca

neb-ee-olo

Few grapes do it for me like Nebbiolo
does, and if Sangiovese is my de Niro,
then Nebbiolo has to be my Pacino!
Much along the lines of great Pinot Noir,
Nebbiolo can be completely awesome,
but also, truly disappointing.

style | This grape's home is in the undoubted food-and-wine heaven that is Piedmont in northwest Italy (*see* f.y.i). The top wines show a combination of concentrated fruit, firm acidity, and a wash of drying tannin. There is very little Nebbiolo outside of Italy, although some brave growers have had limited success in countries such as Australia, New Zealand, and the USA.

taste | Let's concentrate on the really awesome examples for a minute. The best are layered and complex, oozing aromas of tar, roses, dark-cherry, black olive, and rosemary – yes, seriously! This is one of those grape varieties that I can just sit and smell and smell and smell!

f.y.i | So what food should you drink it with? Don't get me started! Nebbiolo is great with a really broad range of food styles, ranging from mushrooms (Piedmont is home to the famous truffle) and chicken, rabbit and all sorts of bizarre and not-so-bizarre types of game, right the way through to really old and mouldy cheeses! The top examples will seriously go the distance if you want to stash a few away.

pinot noir

a.k.a. pinot nero | pineau | savagnin noir | spätburgunder | blauburgunder

pee-no nwar

Pinot Noir is my favourite red grape by a long shot. With more layers than a serious game of Jenga, the truly great examples are seductive, intriguing, even sexy, and their versatility with food is almost unrivalled.

style | Site, climate, yield, and clonal selection all play roles in the success or failure of this variety, considered by many to be the lightest of all red grapes. The Côtes de Nuits, in Burgundy, is its home, where prices of the top examples often have more in common with a new Porsche than they do a bottle of wine! Pinot Noir is also used in Champagne making, where it's blended with Chardonnay and Pinot Meunier. While the southern hemisphere continues to come to terms with it, it's Tasmania as well as Central Otago and Martinborough in New Zealand where Pinot Noir has found places to call home.

taste | At best, Pinot Noir will display layer upon layer of strawberry, raspberry, cherry, and dark-forest fruit, coupled with aromas of earth, spice, animal, cedar, and truffle. In your mouth, Pinot can feel delicate and minerally, or silky and rich, but, in nearly all but a few cases, it will be punctuated by fresh acidity and super-fine tannins.

f.y.i | You don't have to break the bank in order to drink good Pinot Noir, however, being a low-yielding (not producing many grapes), early ripening variety that prefers marginal or cooler climates, you might have to spend a tad more than usual to be dazzled. It's also mega important when purchasing it to pay particular attention to both the region and, most importantly, the producer. If you're unsure, ask the advice of your retailer, as Pinot can be as disappointing as it can be breathtakingly brilliant.

← sangiovese

a.k.a. sangioveto | brunello | prugnolo gentile | morellino | nielluccio

san-gee-o-vay-zee

Robert de Niro would have to rate as one of my all-time favourite actors – classically Italian, super stylish, and the ultimate gangster. By way of comparison, if Tuscan superstar variety Sangiovese were an actor, then it'd be de Niro for sure. Hear me out!

Forgetting the gangster bit, Sangiovese, like de Niro, is also classically Italian and definitely stylish. And just for the record – even though it took some time getting used to – Sangiovese also happens to be one of my favourite grape varieties.

style| Sangiovese is native to Tuscany, where it most obviously shines as Chianti Classico and Brunello di Montalcino. More recently, this variety has surfaced in other parts of the world, including Australia and the USA. However, so far, it hasn't quite had the success abroad that it enjoys in its homeland.

taste | Characteristically loaded with aromas of dark-cherry, plum, and forest fruit, Sangiovese also has a rustic edge, often smelling like tobacco, spice, and earth. Most people best remember Sangiovese for its trademark "super-drying" tannins, which, without the help of food, can make this variety a hard old slog.

f.y.i | Where Sangiovese really comes into its own is when it's paired with the right foods – those tannins work overtime to cut through any grease, fat, and oily textures which provide the base for many Italian dishes.

syrah / shiraz

a.k.a. petite syrah

si-rar / she-raz

So what's the difference? Genetically, Shiraz and Syrah are the same – the differences come in style and origin. The Old World-orientated Syrah tends to be leaner, spicier, and more elegant, while the red superstar of the New World, Shiraz, is often bigger with more fruit, more oak, more everything!

style | North of the equator, Syrah is typically lighter in body than its weightier alter ego, Shiraz, from the southern hemisphere. Well worth a look also are examples from South Africa, Italy, and the USA. But it might be a bit like looking for a needle in haystack, given the microscopic amounts produced in these regions.

f.y.i | Just like Cabernet Sauvignon, Shiraz can cope with some pretty big smelling and flavoured foods, although Syrah has a slight advantage in that, being a tad lighter in style, it can cope with slightly lighter meat dishes and game.

taste | Syrah's characteristics range from redcurrants, raspberry, and plum, with nearly always a super-dooper dose of white pepper and spice. Shiraz boasts intense colour, and at best, oozes smells of dark fruit, raspberry, earth, cedar, and freshly ground pepper. Rich and seamless, its weight and intensity are key features. The power of New World Shiraz fruit is matched by moderate acidity and firm, drying tannin.

a super-dooper dose of
white pepper and spice

tempranillo

tem-pra-nee-o

Spain is currently in the midst of a major wine revolution, and, as the grand old man of the Spanish wine scene, Tempranillo is the local hero. Spain's new school of winemakers is taking a slightly different approach with a recent trend toward bigger "international" styles.

style | Native to Spain's Rioja region, Tempranillo has also sunk its roots in the nearby regions of Ribera del Duero, Navarra, and Priorat. Outside Spain, it has proved its worth, with promising examples popping up in faraway places such as Australia, Chile, and the USA.

taste | Typically, Tempranillo has a solid core of dark-berried fruit, complete with a fairly rustic edge. Traditional examples will often be lighter in colour and more reliant on savoury aromas, such as tobacco, spice, leather, and earth – usually the result of spending extended periods of time in wooden barrels. The more "international" styles flaunt big colour, big fruit, and big oak. These are inky black, with a depth and concentration of dark, dried fruit. And with all the extra weight comes extra tannin, and with Tempranillo we're definitely talking about an adult dose!

f.y.i | As big as it can be, Tempranillo partners up for some classic food-and-wine matches. Roasted meats, particularly beef and lamb, are a must, while its trademark fresh acidity, big fruit, and tannins make this grape brilliant alongside many traditional Spanish casseroles.

↻barbera

bar-bear-a

style | If Nebbiolo is king of Piedmont in Italy's northwest, then Barbera must be the queen. Barbera grows extensively around Italy and on faraway continents alike.

taste | Less rustic, Barbera is bright and cherryish, while nearly always carrying its trademark fresh acidity and low tannins.

f.y.i | Undoubtedly one of my favourite wine stories involves 1950s Australia, when migrating Italian families farmed tobacco. The bottom fell out of the Australian tobacco industry in the late 1970s and many faced no income. The answer? Grape-growing. Victoria has some of the oldest Barbera vines to be found anywhere outside of Italy.

↻cabernet franc
a.k.a. bouchet | grosse vidure

kab-er-nay fronk

style | The grand old daddy of Cabernet Sauvignon! But with the global popularity of Cab Sauv reaching Beatle-mania levels, Cabernet Franc has been relegated to a life of blending. Hailing from Bordeaux in France, it can be found in the Loire, too, and pops up around the globe, such as in Australia, South Africa, and South America.

taste | Sweet and rich, with a great range of aromas and perhaps even more grace than Cab Sauv, the best wines are lush and minerally, jammed full of sweet fruit, and they are really delicious!

f.y.i | Why is it blended? Well, one of its great attributes is its high natural acidity, which provides great backbone for Cabernet-based blends.

↺carignan | a.k.a. carignano | cariñena | mazuelo

car-in-yan

style | Another one of the Sun Lovin' Criminals, Carignan is never more at home than in France. The best results come from the oldest vines, and the Languedoc-Roussillon in France's southwest is home to these. Elsewhere, Carignan has popped up in parts of the USA and in Spain, where it is a permitted blending component in the Tempranillo-based wines of Rioja.

taste | Full-bodied, tannic, and rustic reds... sometimes! But the jury's out as to the worth of this variety. With attributes like "difficult to get ripe" and "highly acidic", there's work to be done.

f.y.i | Once the most widely planted red grape on earth, many Carignan vineyards have been yanked.

↺carmenère

car-man-yeahr

style | I'm a bit of a closet Carmènere lover. But talk to winemakers who have to grow and make the stuff, and more than likely you'll find many of them don't share my enthusiasm. Why? It can be a complete nightmare in the vineyard. Primarily it's hard to get ripe, and then once it is you have a tiny window in which to pick it before the acidity disappears. But when it's good, it's really good!

taste | Bearing an uncanny likeness to Merlot, the best examples burst with dark fruit (think plums, blackberries, and dark-cherries), with aromas of spice and leather – I just can't help myself!

f.y.i | Hailing from Bordeaux, experts and locals believe Carmènere is, in fact, Merlot in disguise.

dolcetto | a.k.a. charbono

doll-chet-o

style | As the everyday drink of Piedmont, Dolcetto ranks after the local king, Nebbiolo, and queen, Barbera. Trying its hardest to appear well-travelled, Dolcetto has found limited success in parts of Australia and the USA.

taste | Often pretty rustic in appearance, aroma, and taste, the trend right now, which is not such a bad thing, is to incorporate the use of micro-oxygenation (the process of pumping microscopic bubbles through the juice during fermentation) to add extra colour, aroma, flavour, and tannin.

f.y.i | Translating as "little sweet one", Dolcetto might one day prove a handy word if you ever happen to find yourself in an Italian singles bar!

gamay | a.k.a. morastrell

gam-may

style | Every year on the third Thursday of November, gazillions of wine-lovers around Europe make the annual pilgrimage to France's Beaujolais region to collect the very first wines of the season, Beaujolais Nouveau. Gamay, while not in massive global demand, is the superstar of Beaujolais, where each year (vintage dependant), it produces wines that are ripe, juicy, and never all that heavy.

taste | These are made using carbonic maceration, a process where grapes are fermented as whole berries and then crushed producing super-fresh wines, with low natural acidity, soft tannins, low alcohol, and best of all, truckloads of ripe, sweet and deliciously raspberryish fruit.

f.y.i | Wines you don't have to think about as you're throwing back your fourth or fifth glass!

mourvèdre | a.k.a. monastrell | mataro

mor-ved-ra

style | Funkier than James Brown and with more farmyard character than Old McDonald could ever handle, Mourvèdre is the bonafide superstar of France's southern Rhône Valley where it makes for a great blending component, especially with varieties such as Grenache and Syrah. In Spain, it's known as both Monastrell and Mataro, while in Australia, it shines under the guise of both Mataro and Mourvèdre.

taste | With all that dark, sweet plum-like fruit there's also mushroom, "animal", tobacco, even mum's roast lamb! Vine age has a huge impact on the overall flavour of this variety, with the older vines producing delicious, inky, full-fruited styles that will soldier on for years and years.

f.y.i | Because of its incredibly funky edge, Mourvèdre is rarely produced as a solo variety and usually reserved as a blender.

negroamaro

neg-ro-maro

style | Southern Italy has a couple of new kids on the block. Alongside Nero d'Avola and Primitivo, Negroamaro (meaning black bitter) is winning the "I'd like mine with balls, please" fans!

taste | The best styles tend to come turbo-charged with smells of tar, morello cherry, Mediterranean spice, and earth. Although it might be too early to tell, the feeling is that varieties such as this might just take to the sunshine of Australia, the USA or perhaps even Chile?

f.y.i | When it comes to food, think big and rich!

⟲ pinotage

pee-no-taj

style | South Africa is firmly divided on this little beast! The value and worth of Pinotage is a super contentious issue in its spiritual home, with many of the Cape's younger winemakers doing their best to forget about it and the legacy that it has left. A hybrid cross between Pinot Noir and Cinsault, Pinotage is probably nothing like what you might imagine, nor what you might expect.

taste | At best, it is ripe, full, dark, and chunky, and requires a fair bit of TLC during its production.

f.y.i | At its worst, it's light, jammy, and bland – good for cleaning heavily-charred barbecues!

⟲ pinot meunier

pee-no moon-yeah

style | The magical third party alongside Chardonnay and Pinot Noir in the Champagne *ménage à trois*! In small doses, Pinot Meunier adds a rich nuttiness that gives weight and intensity to Champagne. Outside France, there are only a handful of places, such as Australia, Germany (where it is known as Samtrot), and New Zealand where plantings of Pinot Meunier can be found. And, although they are made in microscopic quantities, there are a handful of still table wines made from this variety.

f.y.i | Important in the scheme of things it might not be, but I thought that it was still worthy of a mention none the less!

⟳ primitivo / zinfandel

prima-tee-vo

style | The twins! Zinfandel (or Zin) is found in the mighty USA, where all things big are definitely seen as beautiful! It's in California's Napa Valley that Zinfandel has had a long and successful history making incredibly full-fruited styles that come packing a huge punch! Zin becomes Primitivo in Italy's south, particularly Puglia where it holds its head high alongside fellow red varieties, Negroamaro and Nero d'Avola.

taste | With plenty of sweet ripe fruit and aromas of violets and leather, Primitivo's style is much more restrained than the great big head-butt generated from its transatlantic brother, Zin.

f.y.i | For a long time, we kind of assumed that these two kids were distinctly different varieties, but findings from recent research has shown that these grapes are, in fact, twins!

⟳ touriga nacional

too-ree-ga nash-ee-o-narl

style | The king of Portugal's wines, Touriga makes up the basis for many of the great fortifieds of the Douro, and also many of the new-wave table wines. In the same way that Cabernet often needs a partner to soften it up, Touriga can be blended with local versions of Tempranillo.

taste | Deep, densely fruited, leathery, with an almost inky texture, Touriga needs some time to unwind, round out, and mellow. In the table wines, expect to find dried fruit, leather, and violets, while the fortified wines offer rich fruit sweetness and bucket loads of dried fruit and spice.

f.y.i | The wines' richness limits food matches.

11am | Jancis the writer | the words

churning out
thousands of words

every day, in the world of wine Jancis Robinson is to
words what Ferrari is to cars – as good as it gets!

| Charles the owner/activist | the visionary

opportunities in wine were created

by Charles Back long before empowerment projects we[re]
common in South Africa. He continues to do this. Go Cha[rles]

farm
growing grapes

VINEYARDS ARE BASICALLY FARMS, and just like any other fruit farm, this is where grapes are grown and harvested. The name is pretty simple to remember really – take it literally and you have "yards of vines".

This might be an easy way not to get confused with the winery where wine is made, but that's about where the "simple" aspect of the vineyard begins and ends. They are complex and demanding creatures, requiring plenty of attention and all the correct skills to ensure the "right" fruit is produced.

Think of each of the following aspects as a different piece of the puzzle, and you'll begin to understand just how difficult it can be to get each piece in alignment: where to plant your vines; which kind of soil to plant them in; what altitude to plant them at; the best position for your vineyard; how much water to give it; how much sunshine it needs; and how much love, blood, sweat, and tears you're going to have to pour into it.

Keep in mind that, a bit like animals, every vineyard has its own distinct personality or DNA – known in wine circles as terroir (*te-wah*). Terroir is a combination of the environmental and physical factors of a vineyard, including the location, the climate, and the type of soil. A really talented wine professional tasting a glass of wine will, without seeing the bottle, be able to determine which vineyard the wine comes from, because they'll know its distinctive terroir (I'm serious, it is possible).

Together, each of the environmental and physical factors play a huge role in determining how a particular vineyard's grapes will both fare and taste. It's because of the complexity of each of these factors and the many possible combinations of them that, thankfully, no two vineyards are ever exactly the same.

the basic ingredients

Like any recipe, we need to kick things off in the vineyard with a couple of essential basic ingredients. 1 mean things such as climate, soil, and water – all of which are really important when it comes to growing grapes.

And then there's the "X factor". The X factor, or the unpredictable, is Mother Nature, and, as any farmer knows, you can never forget that you are very much at her mercy – she can be as cruel as she can be kind.

Each year will be different from the last, and a different set of seasons from one year to the next will mean that, year in year out, the vineyard will react differently, ultimately affecting the taste of the final wine.

To better understand the process of growing grapes, just imagine we've got a big load of healthy Chardonnay vines to plant, and all we have to do is find them the perfect home. Sound straightforward?

Global positioning, or where we are situated in the world, is the most important consideration before we get busy establishing our vineyard.

If you check out a map of the world, there are only two bands of growing zones where we can plant vines – one band either side of the equator. These growing zones span the 30th and 50th parallels north and south of the equator respectively. Any closer to the equator and you'll be better off growing rice, as conditions are way too hot for growing grapes (the odd exception to the rule is India, whose grape-growers benefit from two harvests a year, thanks to intense heat). Similarly, any further away from the equator and it's too cold, so you'll struggle to get your grapes ripe.

Next on the "DIY Vineyard To Do List" is finding the most suitable...

Climate. As a rule, wines produced north of the equator (or in the northern hemisphere) will be higher in natural acidity and lower in alcohol, while, because of a good dose of sun and possibly a little ozone depletion, the exact opposite (lower acid, higher alcohol) applies to wines in the southern hemisphere.

Try this logic for size: southern hemisphere = more sun; more sun = more fruit, and fruit with a higher sugar content; fruit with a higher sugar content = less acidity and more alcohol (as sugar is what's converted to alcohol during the fermentation process).

Site. Having chosen a suitable climate, finding the perfect site to plant our vines can be about as tricky as trying to ski backward through a revolving door – not impossible (please don't ask for a demo!), but certainly fraught with danger.

there are only two bands of growing zones

where we can plant our vines

Position. To make sure the vines score maximum sunshine hours – essential for photosynthesis and getting our grapes ripe – we need to check that our chosen site is in the right position. Now, if you're planning to stick your vines somewhere in the northern hemisphere, then it's a good idea to have vineyards that face south toward the equator. The opposite applies if you're planting in the south (possibly in sunny Oz!), where north-facing sites are the best.

It's also handy to know that positioning on a hill – where you choose to plant your vines (top or bottom) – will further influence how these grapes end up tasting. As a rule, the higher up your vines are planted, the more acid your grapes will have than those planted lower down, due to progressively cooler growing conditions.

Think snowboarding: snow is more likely to fall at the top of the mountain where it's colder, than at the bottom (and for some of us southern hemisphere folk, it needs to be a seriously good winter before we see any snow!). So, as explained cleverly in the logic trail opposite, colder conditions = fruit with a lower sugar content and, therefore, higher natural acidity.

Let's recap! Geographically, we're in the right part of the world for growing grapes; we've found a suitable climate for our vines; we may even have found the perfect site for the vineyard. The next thing for us to do is find the worst possible soil on that site to plant them in – the very worst you can find!

Soil is really important – from chalk to clay to limestone or granite, even ash – soil plays a massive role in the health of your vines, and to some extent, the final taste of your wine. Some soils drain water better than others, while some are naturally higher in nutrients and minerals. This will determine things such as how much water your vines will get, your vines' ability to retain heat, and even how they will defend themselves against disease. Pretty major stuff!

Water. Vines need water in the same way that any plant does, but not too much as they naturally like to be stressed, so the volume of water they get will have a huge impact on the quality of fruit produced.

Too much water and the vines will be so spoilt they won't work hard enough to produce good fruit, too little and they'll be unable to function. You might need to consider irrigation or manually delivering water to the vines (much the same way you'd water your garden), but if you're really lucky, your vineyard might already be close enough to an underground water source that the vines can easily access via their roots, providing them with all the hydration they need, meaning less work for you, and perhaps more wine-sampling time!

1pm | Philip the buyer | the hunter

as buyer for three busy restaurants

and Australia's largest independently owned wine store,
few great wines make it past Philip without him knowing!

OK, so our vines are finally ready to be planted – I can hear your contented sigh, but I meant it when I said it wasn't simple! You still need to consider how close to plant each vine to its neighbour, how you train them to grow, and finally how you will protect them against disease. This is where you might want to think about doing things following standard practice (fairly straightforward), organically (not so simple), or perhaps even biodynamically (mind-bendingly complex). Here's a brief summary of how they differ.

Conventional viticulture – or growing grapes the good old-fashioned way – is the most common and most commercial practice. This style of grape-growing ensures that the growers have maximum control by allowing them to use whatever they like (within reason, of course) – chemical or otherwise –

to ensure they end up with the best possible result at harvest.

Organic. Fashion aside, this is a popular choice, not only with consumers, but also with grape-growers, who want to get utmost quality out of their vineyards. More and more, you will see wines that have been made from organically grown grapes – grown without the use of industrial fertilizers, herbicides, fungicides, or chemical pesticides. This is gaining momentum, but some growers have shied away from becoming "certified organic" because of the associated politics and complexities. Instead, these growers are content with being "pretty much organic" – not certified but with the flexibility to intervene with non-organic methods should Mother Nature decide to turn against them.

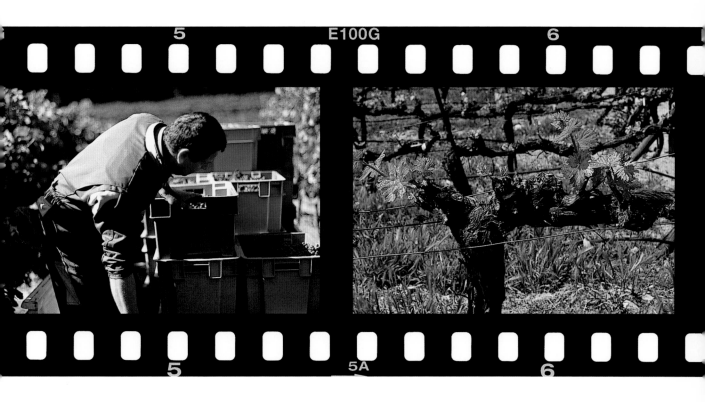

Biodynamic is another can of worms altogether (that's actually funnier than you think!). This practice is very different to organic. Biodynamic viticulture focuses specifically on the production of great wine based on the efforts in the vineyard – efforts that are usually carried out in line with the cycle of the moon. Grape-growers apply various silica (a type of salt) solutions to their vines in a bid to promote health and prevent disease. A good way to think about biodynamic is that it's a bit like naturopathy – only for vineyards.

As a matter of interest, the life span of a vine is roughly the same as that of a human; some live to sixty years, and a handful live beyond 100 years. From the time you stick the baby vines in the ground, it will be five years before they start producing fruit

suitable for wine production (prior to this, the fruit will be highly acidic and green).

With vine age comes maturity and, as a general rule, the older the vines the more concentrated the fruit. As vines get older they become less productive, and although they are producing fruit with incredible concentration, they're producing less of it (think quality not quantity!). Finally, when the vines enter the last phase of their lives, they lose the ability to produce any fruit and will be – brace yourself – yanked from the ground and replaced with a new vine.

Now, with all the major boxes ticked on the "basic ingredients" list: climate, site, soil, water (and planting), you can happily put your feet up, enjoy a glass of wine or three, and ponder what might happen next.

season

This section gives a general idea of "a year in the life of a vineyard". Each season will be subject to a completely different set of weather conditions, the extremities of which will depend on what Mother Nature decides to dish up. Ultimately, this will have a huge effect on the taste and quality of your grapes and, therefore, your wine.

One of the things I truly love about wine is the idea that every single bottle represents "a year in the life of somewhere". I also like the fact that no two growing seasons are ever exactly the same, and dealing with this is a true test of any farmer's skill. Similar to a big game of chess, the best grape-growers are continually reacting, adapting, and trying to pre-empt Mother Nature, in order to grow the best possible grapes. Even in the dodgiest of years, great winemakers still make great wines.

The grape-growing season is like a football year. There's a pre-season, which is spring in the vineyard. Then, it's summer, the proper season, where activity reaches fever pitch. At the end of the season comes the dramatic crescendo in the form of the finals – or the harvest. And then finally, it's all over. The team head off on a well-earned end-of-season trip and drink a lot of beer, while the vines head into winter hibernation. Then, before you know it, three or four months later, the cycle kicks off all over again.

spring

Spring is just about everyone's favourite season. The sun reappears, the air smells fresh and sweet, the birds start to sing again, and you know that summer's just around the corner. Spring is an exciting time in the vineyard. There's an anticipation of the growing season ahead, and how it will shape up is very much determined at this time.

Bud-burst is the most awesome part of spring – the first sign of the vines waking up from hibernation. This is when the tiny green buds appear on, what still look like, lifeless vines. The buds will eventually become vine canes complete with their own leaves, tendrils, and grapes. But, of course, with any good comes the threat of bad, and, in spring, that means frost in the vineyard.

Frost, which can also occur in summer and autumn, can completely devastate a vineyard, especially one full of new growth. When the temperature drops below zero degrees, the frost freezes the buds from the inside out. They are unable to recover from this, and will sadly brown and die.

There are methods to protect against frosts, from ultra-expensive helicopter fly-bys (that blow away large masses of cold air), to vineyard heaters that turn freezing air into water before it's had a chance to settle. But the most common and cost effective method are sprinkler systems, which, once the temperature reaches a particular low point, spray the buds with a light coating of water. This freezes around the outside of the bud, stopping the really cold air from infiltrating – kind of like an igloo for vines!

Vineyard DIY. Spring is the time to get handy in the vineyard, with all sorts of maintenance and repairs, such as trellising and fencing. Spring is the time for planting new vine cuttings, and for trimming any unwanted foliage from existing vine canes, so that all of their energy can be focused on the buds – the first sign of new baby grapes.

Having made it safely through spring, summer breathes new life into the vineyard.

2pm | Jan the vineyard manager | the labourer

the world's first Fairtrade wine

was made by Thandi estate. Jan Jaanson is carer of the fruit here – he sees his job as contributing to the future of the community.

summer

Summer in the vineyard brings with it a flurry of activity.

Flowering occurs roughly ten days after bud-burst. The flowers eventually transform into bunches of grapes. Once the bunches have formed (fruit set), most grape-growers insure themselves by spraying some kind of pesticide and fungicide that will protect the vine from disease during the most critical time – the 100 days of ripening.

Veraison occurs after seventy days or so. This is when a grape enters the final phase of ripening and changes colour.

Ripeness. When are the grapes ripe enough to pick? One handy option is a little machine that tests sugar and acidity levels. But many seasoned campaigners claim that the most foolproof way of checking ripeness is to simply taste the fruit, looking for "physiological ripeness", where the entire grape is ripe: skins, stalks, and pips included. If sugar levels in the grapes are too high (which can happen very quickly in a warm climate or hot weather), the resulting wines can become too alcoholic. Likewise, if the grapes are not ripe enough (a risk in a wet, cool year), the wines can be thin and acidic.

Harvest is a nerve-racking time for wine producers, with all of their beautiful ripe fruit sitting vulnerably on the vines. Think of it as their annual salary literally hanging there – a year's income that can easily be consumed by hungry birds, or decimated by a hailstorm in a matter of minutes.

Most grapes nowadays are harvested by a machine, which don't complain about the heat, don't stop for lunch, and don't charge by

the hour! But the good old-fashioned way is for teams of pickers to work through two or even three "selections" to ensure that all of the grapes are at maximum quality and perfect ripeness when picked. Hands are also kinder on the fruit, compared with the machines, which smack the grapes from the vines with the force of Bruce Lee, and, inevitably, cause damage. Last of all, machines can't always get where people can. Once picked, it's crucial that the grapes are transported as quickly and as gently as possible to the winery, to limit general damage and deterioration of the fruit due to contact with oxygen.

autumn

In the winery, autumn continues to be a hive of activity. It is also the season of recovery – well, for the pickers at least! Harvest is hard work. Days are long and usually pretty hot, too. All you can really think about is sitting under that big old shady tree drinking beer and snoozing for the rest of the afternoon. Then you accidentally cut yourself for the first time. You look up and try to stretch, realizing that your back is aching. You're not even half done for the day, and there's still three weeks of picking ahead! So it's great relief to the pickers that autumn sees the end of the harvest, and the end of harvest means a harvest party!

Toward the latter part of this season, the vines' leaves begin to change colour and, eventually, fall off. This is one of the most beautiful times in any vineyard – rows of vines become blankets of incredible yellows, oranges, and reds. The air begins to get cooler and you can almost smell winter lurking around the corner.

winter

All the leaves are gone and the sky is grey... Yep, sadly winter is the quietest season in the vineyard. The vines head into hibernation for a well-earned rest, while most of the grape-growers escape for a well-deserved holiday.

Pruning. Winter is when pruning for the coming year begins. This is the process where the canes are trimmed back in order to make way for next year's new growth. This can be a gruelling task for the pruners, who brave the elements in order to give the vines a great big haircut.

And while nothing much is going on outside in the vineyard, all of the really serious activity is taking place behind closed doors not too far away in the winery...

CT8/33-8

KOD'AK 400TX

53

the end of harvest means a
harvest party!

production
making wine

WINE IS MADE IN THE WINERY. You get big wineries, small ones, old and dusty ones, even brand spanking new ones. And inside the winery is where it all happens. I love going to wineries. Some of my earliest memories are of visiting them as a kid with my mum and dad. And, although back then it wasn't me doing the tasting, I was still mesmerized by the smell of fermenting wine and wood, the seemingly endless rows of wooden barrels, and all those gigantic stainless-steel tanks – each one looking as though it might be capable of holding a small ocean! If you've ever been inside the doors of a winery, you'll know exactly what I'm talking about.

Let's just quickly recap where we were in the vineyard before moving onto production in the winery. Grapes are picked once they're ripe (that's a pretty succinct summary of the last chapter, isn't it?), and the next step in the chain is delivering the grapes to the winery where they'll be processed. Converting grape juice into wine is a simple procedure. The art of making really great wine is something far more involved.

Think of wineries as care homes for grapes, and the role of the winemaker as being to nurse the fruit through the production process; the skill lies in not messing with the fruit too much that it no longer tastes of where it comes from. As logical and easy as all this sounds, it's not. It takes a huge amount of both experience and skill to capture and preserve what we referred to earlier as "terroir", or regional identity (see p.87) – the distinctive characteristics of the vineyard naturally ingrained in its grapes.

As always, there's an exception, and not all wines end up being reflective of their origins or terroir, and nor do they have to be. In order to meet demand and sometimes to sidestep Mother Nature, many bigger companies, that need to consistently turn out massive volumes of wine, are often forced to source grapes from a number of different areas, and even countries. This is known as multi-regional blending, and it's not a bad thing so long as the wine is well made.

So how is wine made?

in the winery

Once the grapes enter the winery, the number of directions the winemaker can take are endless, depending on the colour and style of wine to be made, and the individual preferences and abilities of the winemaker. Some like to chill the grapes immediately to preserve flavours in the fruit (fermenting at different temperatures will capture or highlight different flavours in the grapes). Others will sort through the grapes again, to remove any sub-standard berries that may have slipped through.

Fermentation is the one factor common to all wine, irrespective of variety or style. It is the process of converting grape juice into wine, and the principals of fermentation are the same regardless of whether it's beer, wine, or spirits you're making – or even bread. The basic process goes like this: we begin with a raw product that contains natural sugar, which our grape juice does.

Yeast is then added, or naturally introduces itself to the juice, where it acts a bit like Pac-Man, munching up the natural sugar and converting it into alcohol. The by-product of fermentation is carbon dioxide, which is continuously released. When the grape is picked, around 12 per cent is natural sugar. After fermentation, the juice will be 12 per cent alcohol, but it's no longer grape juice; it's now wine.

There are two types of yeast: cultured and wild. Cultured yeast comes in a powdered form (think instant soup mix), and is simply added to the grape juice by the winemaker, where like clockwork it starts fermenting, continues fermenting, and – you guessed it –

finishes fermenting. Just as it says it will on the pack. Cultured yeast offers most control over the fermentation. There is no risk of the ferment "sticking" (randomly stopping midway through the process), and cultured yeasts will almost certainly guarantee trouble-free winemaking. This type of yeast is particularly good for big volumes of wine and large-scale commercial production.

Wild yeast is a mutated strain of cultured yeast (a bit like the starter you'd use for sourdough bread) that lives naturally in a particular environment. Think about these guys as kind of like the "Hell's Angels" of the yeast world. It is very different to cultured yeast; wild yeast doesn't come out of a packet and it most certainly doesn't come with a set of instructions. Instead, the winemaker waits for the yeast to introduce itself to the grape juice (the yeast naturally seeks out sugar in any form), and then hopes (praying helps, too!) it behaves once it does.

Wild yeast is notorious for randomly "sticking", a nightmare scenario that often requires around the clock supervision. The major benefit is that it should add extra dimension to the wine – something that cultured yeast could never contribute.

Depending on the grape variety and style of wine to be produced, the winemaking process can be broken down into the following basic steps.

how to make white wine

Once white grapes – or any grapes for that matter – hit the winery, they are nearly always crushed and de-stemmed before anything else. A machine is used to gently split the grapes and remove the stalks and stems from each bunch. The reason for this (and eventually removing the skins and pips) is that they contain bitter and astringent tannins, which are okay in reds, but only rarely in whites.

Sulphur dioxide will most likely be added then to stop fermentation kicking off and to stop the wine from turning brown and tasting like vinegar (oxidation). Allergies to SO_2 are quite common and, as a result, there are "sulphur-free" wines available. But these wines have a fairly limited life span, so you'll want to drink them pretty quickly.

The press. The split grapes are then pressed to capture their juice. Modern examples of presses are huge mechanical beasts. Inside is a gigantic canvas balloon that gently inflates, squashing the grapes. The juice escapes through small holes in the sides, while skins, pips, and other unwanted bits are separated and retained within the press.

The development of the wine press is one area where technology has allowed winemakers to make much better wines, especially whites. The old-school style of grape press was similar to the above: cylindrical, but made from wooden slats and much less sophisticated. Grapes were placed inside the press and the lid was then "screwed" down on top of the fruit with the juice being forced through the wooden slats.

This kind of press is still used today, and is great for big gutsy reds that require a lot of colour and tannin (obtained from the skins and pips through forceful pressing), but it's definitely not a flash method for whites where only the juice is wanted.

Once pressed, the white grape juice is lightly pumped (it doesn't like being pushed too hard) into a connecting stainless-steel tank. The juice is then left to allow any floating bits to settle at the bottom of the tank, where they can be left behind. The juice is then gently transferred into another tank (for unwooded wines), or wooden barrels (for wooded). Fermentation then begins (using the preferred yeast type), and can last from three to thirty days.

unwooded whites

Once the white wine has finished fermenting, it will be "racked", or removed from the stainless-steel tank, at which point the dead yeast cells, or lees, deposited as a result of fermentation, will be left behind.

Aromatic whites, such as Riesling and Gewurztraminer, are, in nearly all cases, fermented and stored in stainless-steel tanks until filtration and bottling. The exception to this rule can be found in much of Europe, where both the above-mentioned varieties are stored in huge wooden casks. If you look inside these casks, you will see a crust of tartaric crystals (tartaric acid is found naturally in grapes and their juice in which it solidifies) naturally deposited from wines over time. This coating acts kind of like cling film, ensuring no oak character from the casks are imparted into the wine. Why use them? Purely as a storage vessel.

Sauvignon Blanc is also mostly produced without the influence of oak (there are oaked examples in France's Loire Valley and the USA). In Australia, especially the west, you'll often find blends of Sauvignon Blanc and Semillon, in which either all or part of the Semillon component has spent some time in wood. Speaking of Semillon, if you get the chance, try the amazing old examples from Australia's Hunter Valley.

Traditionally, these wines are produced without even a sniff of oak, but, after an extended period of time in the bottle, they take on a beautiful, toasty, nutty character tricking the taster into believing they had seen at least a smidge of wood.

Chardonnay is one of those white varieties that can swing either way. Good-value, unwooded Chardonnay is hugely popular around the globe, although, as a rule, the best examples of this variety nearly always spend some time in wood. There are exceptions, and winemakers in France's Chablis (*shab-lee*) district are the masters of producing complex, minerally, and super long-lived examples without the use of oak. The ancient chalky soil of Chablis requires winemaking to be completely unadulterated, simple, and straightforward, in order to preserve its crystal-clear regional character.

The major benefit of unwooded whites is, aside from being relatively cheap to produce, they require no work after fermentation and can be bottled ready for release quickly.

and wooded whites…

A handful of "bigger" white varieties love a bit of time in wood. The use of oak adds complexity and a framework to what might otherwise be a simple, one-dimensional wine, lacking structure and the ability to age.

Wooded wines can go through their primary (first) fermentation in stainless-steel tanks before being transferred to oak barrels to either finish fermenting, or, if desired, they can go through a secondary fermentation, known as malolactic fermentation. Try saying that three times quickly after a couple of glasses of wine! Another option is to ferment your wine from start to finish in oak, which is called "barrel fermentation".

Brace yourselves; here comes another quick science lesson! If you weren't sure, MLF (malolactic fermentation) sounds like it could be a major financial institution – even an '80s rock band – but it's not! It's actually the process whereby the malic acid in wine (think tart Granny Smith apples) is transferred into lactic acid (think milk). MLF occurs towards the end of the fermentation process via the addition of bacteria where it not only softens the acidity of a wine, but also gives it those creamy, buttery characters. This process occurs naturally in all red wines, but has to be kick-started in whites where it is usually only employed in varieties such as Chardonnay and Sémillon, softening undrinkably high acidity and producing smells of butterscotch and cream. Wooded whites can spend anywhere from six to twelve months soaking in oak before being transferred to tank for filtration.

wooded whites
can spend anywhere from six to twelve months soaking in oak

Filtration or fining. It's kind of like the process of giving the wine a good spit and polish to get it ready for bottling. The most traditional method of fining is to drop an egg white solution into the wine; the mixture falls through the wine acting like a net, capturing any suspended particles or impurities (the most common being dead yeast cells). On the more commercial side, large volumes of wine are usually fined via a membrane filter – imagine a big sieve made up of a number of finely perforated sheets. Some winemakers will shy away from filtering altogether, believing it will strip the wine of characters developed during the winemaking process.

Once the wine has been fined, it will be bottled and sealed, ready for sale, and, more importantly, ready for drinking! Now, speaking of seals, unless you've been living

in a bubble for the past few years, you'll be aware of the super-sized debate that's been simmering away over the use of the screwcap (a.k.a. Stelvin closure) versus the traditional cork.

Cork closures. At the time of writing, it's estimated that somewhere between five and seven per cent of all wine bottled with a traditional cork will be spoilt by TCA (2,4,6-Trichloroanisole), a type of bacteria that thrives in cork and is every winemaker's worst nightmare. Have you ever tasted a wine that reminded you of damp cardboard or a musty room? The chances are it had been infiltrated by the evil TCA. Looking at the current rate, it seems as if the efforts of the cork manufacturers to clean up their act may be a matter of too little, too late. Another problem with corks is the effect of random oxidation (the premature ageing of wine due to excess oxygen contact).

Synthetic closures, or plastic corks, are an alternative closure, but even they are not without their problems. While plastic corks eliminate the problem of cork taint, what's inside can still be ruined thanks to a leaky seal (causing the wine to oxidize). Worse still, plastic corks can be very tricky to remove, and there's nothing more frustrating than looking forward to a glass of wine and not being able to open the bottle!

The screwcap. Not surprisingly, winemakers are desperate, and have explored nearly every possible alternative closure – enter the screwcap. Romantic they're not, but screwcaps more or less guarantee that your wine will taste as the winemaker intended. Surely that's a good thing – they even force winemakers to make better wines. Love them or hate them, I'm pretty sure that screwcaps are going to be with us for some time.

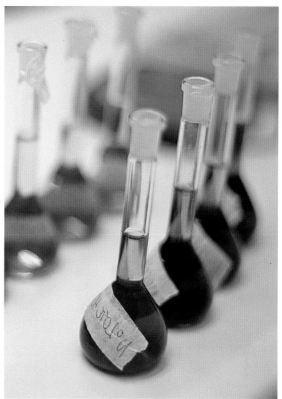

and what about rosé?

With a foot in each camp, rosé is a red wine that's made as though it's a white wine. The first part of its production is straightforward and follows the same basic steps of white wine production – that is, right up to the point where you throw the skins in with the juice. The skins? Yep, the skins!

Squeeze a red grape between your fingers and you'll discover that the juice is clear. As you'll find out next, red wine takes its colour from its skins, as does rosé. The trick with rosé is to leave the skins in contact with the juice for only a short period of time, allowing a small amount of colour extraction (pink!), together with the faintest lick of tannin.

The addition of skins is the most common rosé method, but others include blending a small amount of red wine into white wine.

rosé is a red wine
that's made as though it's a white wine

how to make red wine

The main difference between red and white wine production is the addition of the skins (and sometimes stalks, too) in the red winemaking process. Skins, pips, and stalks provide red wine with colour, structure, and a small amount of flavour.

As with white grapes, red grapes are initially crushed and de-stemmed. The stalks are removed at this point, because unless they're really woody and ripe, they will give off bitter and astringent characters – not good! The exception is with Pinot Noir, where winemakers often include a percentage of stalks to give bonus flavour to the wines (but only if they're woody and ripe).

Colour and flavour. The cocktail of grape skins and juice is transferred after crushing to open-topped tanks, which can be made of wood, stainless-steel, or concrete. Once fermentation begins, the build up of carbon dioxide (remember the by-product of fermentation) will push the skins to the top of the tank (whihc is then known as the cap). But to extract the colour and flavours locked in the skins, they need to be continually mixed with the juice.

How, I hear you ask? Well, let me explain!

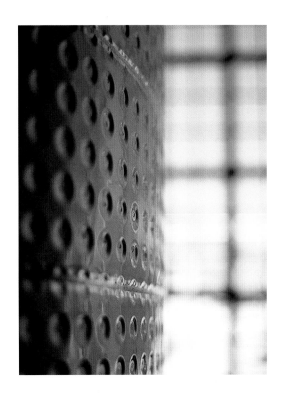

keeping the cap down

Back in the good old days, workers would hop nude into the tanks and push the cap down with their legs. Not only was this process physically exhausting, but potentially fatal (yep, fatal!). This wasn't from the risk of drowning, but due to the high levels of carbon dioxide given off during fermentation. As you can probably appreciate, regulations have ensured that this method has effectively been globally outlawed.

Pigeage. Other less hazardous methods include "pigeage" (*pee-garge*), the French term for using a long broom-like device to manually push the skins back down into the juice – again physically exhausting work.

Pumping over is a far more common (and, thankfully, easier) method. All that's needed are a couple of hoses and a pump – sounds fairly straightforward, doesn't it? Stick one of the hoses into the tank, connect it to the pump, and hang on as the juice is then forced through the second hose which is used to "water" the cap. As the juice passes through the cap, the skins, colour, and tannins are extracted. This also keeps the cap moist, which is important if you don't want your wine turning to vinegar.

Roto-fermenters. Modern technology has meant that much of this process has now been automated. Roto-fermenters, generally found in bigger wineries, are large spinning tanks that mix both the cap and juice together in a bid to maximize the extraction of colour and tannin – a little bit like a food processor for the winemaker!

Whichever method is used, the process is usually carried out several times a day, depending on the amount of extraction the winemaker wants, and is continued until primary fermentation has finished.

3pm | Liberty Wines the sales team | the sellers

selling to 1,000s of London restaurants

this team has its work cut out. But, at the end of the day there's nearly always something liquid to enjoy!

oak can be given a whole range of seasonings
and flavours

one last squeeze

As with white wine, it's only the "clean" red wine that is transferred to either tank or barrel. What's left in the bottom of the fermentation tank (whole grapes, skins, and pips) will be separately transferred back to the press for a good old squeeze to wring out any remaining juice.

This extracted juice will be super-rich in colour and tannin, and can be used as a valuable blending component, but is definitely not fit for consumption on its own.

Most red wines, with a handful of exceptions, spend anywhere from six months to two years in oak barrels of varying age, make, and size. So why oak then?

why oak?

Oak has been used in wine production forever and a day, not only for its flavour properties, but also for its credentials as a watertight storage vessel.

Barrels are also easy to move – even when full, they'll roll without much effort. Most of the oak used now comes from either the forests of France or the USA, though there are small oak productions in Slovenia, South America, and Australia. All give distinctly different characteristics, but the most important consideration when choosing oak is the cooper it comes from.

The cooper is someone who harvests the wood, cuts it, dries it, and then fashions the oak staves – either by fire or steam – into barrels. Oak can be given a whole range of seasoning or flavours before it is assembled into barrels. This seasoning process will have an effect on the final flavours in your wine, and it's for this reason that many producers prefer to use older wooden barrels in an effort not to have excessive real oak character imparted into their wines. Oak also plays a major structural role in the production of red wine. Oak, like grape skins, contains tannins – wood tannins. These wood tannins are slightly harsher than those found in grape skins, but are essential, as they help to stabilize both the colour of a wine and the overall tannin structure. The last point on oak is that it's not cheap, and usually ends up being the major annual outlay for most wineries.

Oak chips. In order to save on production costs, some winemakers will use oak chips in their wine to impart the oaky character. This is done by suspending a kind of big tea bag filled with chipped-up old barrels in the tank, which will impart those desirable woody characteristics into the wine in a relatively short space of time.

The finale. After the ageing period, the wine will be transferred from barrel back to tank, where prior to filtering, it may be racked (moving the wine from one tank to another to leave any nasties behind).

Finally, the wine is filtered (as with white wine) and bottled. In most cases, the bottled wine will be kept back at the winery, where it will rest for a specified period (anywhere from three to twelve months) prior to release.

Bottling lines, like wineries, come in all shapes and sizes. Smaller bottling lines are mobile, and specifically cater for tiny production or producers, who can't afford the luxury of installing their very own bottling line.

how to make fizzy wine

Hands up if you like fizzy wine! That's all of you! Sparkling wine, by definition, is any wine that is saturated with carbon dioxide (bubbles) under pressure (a bottle). And there's a number of different ways of getting all those bubbles in there in the first place...

Sparkling wine and Champagne are most commonly made from Chardonnay, Pinot Noir, and Pinot Meunier. They are both basically the same thing, the main difference being their place of origin. By law, only those wines coming from the region of Champagne in France are allowed to be called "Champagne". If you don't want to look like a complete novice, and out of respect for French Champagne makers, it's really important that you remember this.

So, for sparkling wines or Champagne, you need to start with a "base wine". Base wines are usually pretty horrible to taste, as they're purposely made from highly acidic grapes. Then there are several methods available to get bubbles into the base wine.

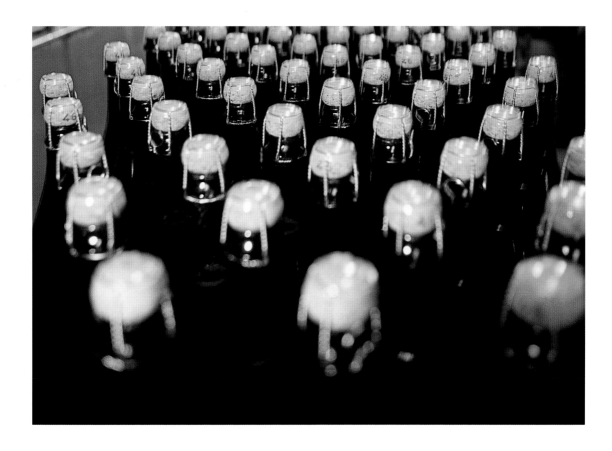

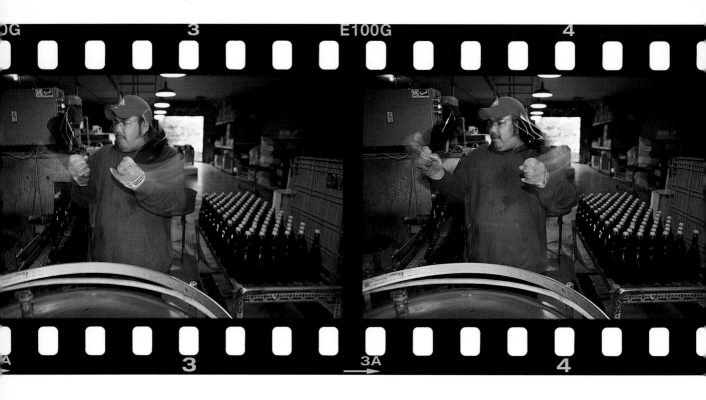

getting bubbles into wine

Carbonation, the cheapest method, is the same one that you would use to make a can of soft drink. Carbon dioxide is pumped into a tank full of wine, which is then bottled under pressure to stop the gas from escaping – also known as the "bicycle pump" method. The cheapest wines are made this way.

The Transfer Method is used to produce large volumes of low- to medium-priced sparkling wine. A sweetened base wine has yeast added to it and a second fermentation takes place in an enclosed tank, so that the carbon dioxide can't escape. When the fermentation is finished, the wine is clarified, re-sweetened or blended if necessary, and then bottled (again under pressure to retain the gas).

When a wine has undergone a second fermentation in bottle, it is known as *Méthode Champenoise*. Generally speaking, this produces the best quality wines.

Méthode Champenoise goes like this: the primary fermentation can take place in either large, temperature-controlled stainless-steel vessels, or smaller oak barrels, although the use of oak is much less common. Once the first

fermentation is finished, the wines generally go through malolactic fermentation. This is where the winemaker puts together his jigsaw puzzle, using hundreds of different batches of fermented wine at his disposal, from not only different grape varieties, but also different vintages. The batches are then blended together at the winemaker's discretion and transferred into sealed bottles with an additional mixture of liqueur called "*liqueur de tirage*" (usually cane sugar mixed with some of the wine) and yeast. This process allows a second fermentation to take place in the bottle, with the resulting carbon dioxide trapped underneath the seal.

Many of the flavours in the sparkling wine are derived from the contact it has with the dead yeast cells. This is known as yeast autolysis, which imparts characteristic toast, brioche, and Vegemite characters. Mmmm Vegemite! The dead yeast cells form a deposit

in the bottom of the bottle, and need to be removed to get the Champagne looking its best for sale. This is achieved by riddling, or "*remuage*", where the bottles are placed horizontally in wooden racks and each day they're turned an eighth and tilted until they're vertically positioned upside down. This process causes all of the unwanted sediment to be trapped in the neck of the bottles. The neck of the bottle, and its contents, are then frozen by dipping them into a very cold brine solution.

Disgorgement or "*dégorgement*" (no, it's not some sort of gladiator battle) is next. The seals on the bottles are removed and the pressure of the built-up gas forces the frozen sediment out. The bottles are then topped up with some sugary wine, or "*liqueur d'expédition*" to offset the high acidity of the base wine, corks are inserted and wired, and it is finally ready for sale.

how to make sweet wine

Sweet wines are a bit like drummers – technically brilliant, but underrated and too often overshadowed by the rest of the band. And like drummers, for most dessert wines that are stuck at the back of a wine list, it's a case of "out of sight, out of mind".

Add to this the fact that many sweet wines are super pricey, which is mainly down to mega production costs, and you find that most people give them a big miss. Just imagine a world without the talents of John Bonham, Meg White, or even Ringo for that matter! Shudder...

The number of ways to produce sweet wine is dizzying. It can be a really costly process, as, essentially, you're hyper-concentrating the sugar in your grapes while at the same time removing the natural water content. Here, we explore the most common methods.

Bubblicious. Sweet fizzy wines might be few and far between, but these wines highlight the range of diversity in relation to production. Moscato d'Asti is the most obvious example of this style and it hails from Italy's northwest.

Served icy cold, Moscato is an incredibly light and slightly fizzy wine that is low in alcohol (5 degrees – good for your conscience, your waistline, and means you can drink twice as much!) with plenty of fresh and zippy apple and pear flavours.

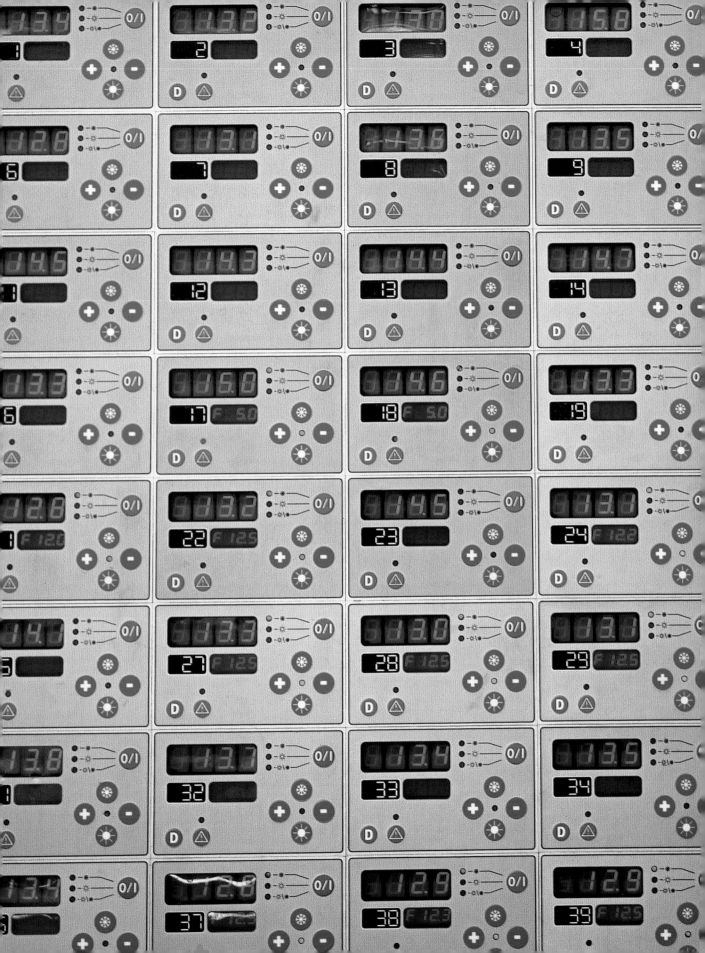

Moscato is generally made using the Transfer Method – the same process incorporated in the production of many mid-range sparkling wines described previously. The Moscato juice is placed in a giant airtight tank where fermentation begins. Once the alcohol strength reaches around 5 degrees, the temperature is rapidly dropped to kill off the fermentation process. As with any sparkling wine made using the transfer method, carbon dioxide is trapped in the tank and forced to saturate the wine making it lightly fizzy.

Let them rot. *Botrytis cinerea* is an airborne spore (picture a microscopic back-to-front flying trumpet) that attacks grapes in humid conditions with little natural airflow. These trumpets suck out the water from the grapes, concentrating their sugar levels.

Now, before you think that botrytis can occur anywhere, it can't! Many grape-growers deliberately plant vineyards in areas with little ventilation and close proximity to water in order to try to attract botrytis infection. But even that's not enough. There's a number of different types of rot, and not all of them will give your wine attractive botrytis-like characters. Getting your grapes to rot and go mouldy is seriously hard work!

In the French region of Sauternes, where botrytis thrives providing the world with some of the greatest sweet wines made anywhere, the key to making fantastic wine is individual grape selection.

In the best vineyards, pickers will revisit the same bunches again and again to ensure optimum fruit ripeness and level of infection prior to picking. Sub-standard grapes will be removed from bunches with nail scissors – how's that for extreme attention to detail?

Once in the winery, the production process is fairly straightforward. The grapes are pressed and the juice is fermented in the usual way before being transferred into brand new oak for an extended period of time.

Hung out to dry. Sweet wines made from air-dried grapes – most common to Italy – are usually made in minute quantities. The production process is long, difficult, and costly. In a nutshell, grapes are harvested and then taken to an open-sided drying room, where whole bunches are laid out on drying racks. These racks allow for oxygen flow, which, together with the open-sided drying room, ensure the grapes are not subjected to any form of rot.

The environment is kept as dry as possible, with small fires being lit regularly to compensate for any rise in humidity. This process requires a monster amount of skill and patience.

After three months or so, bunches are transferred to the press, where, having been reduced by around two-thirds of their original size, they are squashed. The freshly squeezed and extra-sugary juice is then transferred to small wooden barrels which are cemented shut.

The wine will then begin to ferment – a dangerous stage of the production process as the carbon dioxide can only escape slowly via the pores in the wood. The big worry here is that if there's an excessive build-up of carbon dioxide inside the barrel, it can easily explode. But, all things going to plan, and after an extended period of ageing (usually around three or so years), the wine will have reduced by a significant amount due to natural evaporation.

At this point, it will be freshened up with some newer wine and finally bottled ready for sale, usually just under five years after the grapes were first picked!

this process requires **a monster amount of skill and patience**

4pm | Raeleen the cellar door manager | the face

pouring dozens of samples for visitors

at Rockford winery in Australia's Barossa Valley, Raeleen
meets, greets, and sells, and has done for over twelve years.

That's the spirit! Currently not as popular as they were thirty years ago, fortified wines are going through a difficult time, but there is light at the end of the tunnel.

Port comes from a beautiful area in northern Portugal (think about the name and it'll make sense) called the Douro Valley, where more than eighty grape varieties are allowed in the production process.

The fermentation process is much the same as for dry red wine. However, the fermentation is prevented from finishing by the addition of brandy spirit, which increases the alcoholic strength up to around 18 degrees. This level of alcohol kills the fermenting yeasts and the result is a super sweet wine with a super high alcohol content!

In Australia, fortified wine (not port as it doesn't come from Portugal) is generally made from red variety Shiraz, while in the south of Spain, white variety Pedro Ximénez is transformed over time into a syrupy rich fortified style known as "black sherry". Lighter perfumed Muscats are also made in Spain and the Rhône Valley in France.

The lack of airplay that these wines get is a bit of a shame really, as they make such great partners to a really broad range of foods. Port is never more at home than with a big wedge of blue cheese, while both Aussie and Spanish fortifieds alike lend themselves to everything from nuts, Christmas pudding, and chocolate!

JACOBS CREEK

atlas
where it happens

**GREAT WINE IS MADE EVERYWHERE –
IT'S THAT SIMPLE!** As consumers, we tend to be incredibly parochial drinkers, usually playing it safe and sticking to what we know, which, more often than not, means drinking wines from our own country. But the best wine producers are rarely concerned with what's going on in their own backyard, they're usually far more concerned with who's making the best examples using similar varieties to their own, and more importantly, how they're doing it. This is what sets great winemakers apart from the pack. I reckon it's a pretty good attitude – perhaps we could adopt a similar approach in the way we consume wine...

Now, as we mentioned in the Farm chapter, you can pretty much slice the planet into two major growing zones north and south of the equator. The northern zone encompasses Italy, France, Germany, Spain, Portugal, and North America, while the major countries incorporated into the southern zone include Australia, New Zealand, South Africa, and South America.

Last little lecture before we get down to business: one of the dangers that the great big world of wine faces is the global homogenization of wine; wines that are more influenced by winemaking techniques than by where they're from. Don't get me wrong, if the wine is well-made, then that's great, but surely it's all going to get a bit boring when Cabernet from Italy looks like Cabernet from Chile and South Africa and France, and so on and so on. You get my drift. The most important thing for grape-growers and winemakers alike is to focus regional varieties and concentrate on making them well. That's where the real challenge lies.

Take yourself outside of your comfort zone, if you know you like Cabernet Sauvignon from Australia, why not check out some of the awesome examples of Cabernet from Chile or South Africa? Sure they're all going to be a bit different at first, but isn't that a good thing? The world of wine is a very small place and it's right there waiting for you to explore!

up north – north of the equator

North of the equator is kind of like Disneyland for wine-lovers. Bringing together the traditional growing areas of Europe alongside the vineyards of North America, the northern hemisphere is a melting pot of climatic diversity and style. With the exception of North America, much of the grape-growing area that falls north of the Equator is known as the "Old World". Just about forever, the term "Old World" has referred to old practices, old winemaking techniques, old ways of thinking about pretty much everything to do with wine. That is, until now...

italy

Great coffee, the best pizza, swanky clothes, awesome football, and very fast cars. When it comes to enjoying life to the extreme, Italians do it better than just about anyone else. And while quantity doesn't always walk hand in hand with quality, recent times have seen Italy – the world's largest producer of wine by volume – do a major about-face in the quality department. Gone is the reputation as a manufacturer of cheap and nasty Lambrusco, and in its place lies new-found identity as a high-quality producer of regionally influenced wines.

Climatically, Italy is a land of extremes, and, as a result, produces wines that vary greatly in character depending on which end of the boot they're from. The further north you go, the cooler it gets, translating into generally lighter wines with bucket loads of elegance and finesse. This is also where Italy's best whites come from. Head way down south toward Sicily and you'll notice things change dramatically. Still very much Italian, it's as though the wines have been turbo-charged! Big colour, big smell, and monster flavours are the rule. Here are my top Italian regions.

5pm | Matt, Chris, and Bob the wine generation | the family

ambassadors for wine in their region,

local producers are insanely passionate about regional identity, and are firmly committed to the area's future.

Piedmont. To say that I love this, Italy's northwestern-most wine region, almost sells it short. Hear me out. The Piedmont region personifies food and wine culture like nowhere else in the world – I never get tired of going back. Let's just say that if heaven turns out to be anything like Piedmont (home of the white truffle), then that's cool with me. But it's not just the food and wine, it's the people, too. If Tuscany's personality is about big, bold, concentration, and aristocracy, then Piedmont, by way of comparison, is all about elegance, purity, refinement, and family.

Home to red varieties like Barbera and Dolcetto, it's the temperamental superstar, Nebbiolo, which rules the roost here, consistently cranking out some of the most seductive, intriguing, and sexy examples of wine assembled anywhere on the planet. There are white varieties here, too, such as Cortese (Gavi di Gavi), Arneis, and Moscato, surely one of the world's most underrated sweet wines (*see also* p.58, 122, 124).

Trentino-Alto Adige. It's fair to say that Italy is better known for the quality of its reds than its whites, but among the chilly hills of this region, located in the northeastern corner of Italy at the base of the Dolomites, lie some of Italy's best examples of aromatic white varieties: Pinot Grigio and Gewürztraminer; and Pinot Noir which lends itself to making great sparkling wine. Head south and one of the smaller wine-producing areas, Friuli-Venezia Giulia, is producing some of the most off-the-wall wines with white varieties such as Pinot Bianco, Chardonnay, and Sauvignon Blanc.

Tuscany. With images of huge old villas, sprawling vineyards, great food, better wine, Florence, and some of the most picturesque countryside to be found anywhere in the world, it's no wonder that Tuscany is regarded today as not only the most important wine region in Central Italy, but perhaps also the measuring stick for food and wine tourism worldwide.

Sangiovese is the superstar red variety of Tuscany, where it shows up as Chianti Classico, Chianti Rufina, Chianti Colli Senesi, and Brunello di Montalcino. The prime spot for growing Sangiovese is the famed Concadoro (the golden shell), located smack in the middle of Chianti Classico.

The South. Currently, there's lots of excitement surrounding what is going on south of Rome. Essentially, the bulk of wine from the south comes from the area of Puglia, and the islands of Sicily and Sardinia. While much of the south's production is consumed in Italy, there are a handful of new-school producers who have had some international success with varieties such as Negroamaro, Nero d'Avola, and Primitivo. Watch this space!

The wines, most of which are red, tend to be inkier in style than those up north, and loaded with masses of sun-drenched fruit and sweet Mediterranean spice.

france

As the most diverse and important wine-producing country in the world, France is the Holy Grail of wine – the original soul brother. Every winemaker around the globe, whether they like to admit it or not, has, at some stage, taken influence from the very best wines of France. Home to the much-famed regions of Bordeaux, Burgundy, and Champagne to name but a few, the following include the most important wine-producing regions in France.

Bordeaux is the largest wine-producing area in France with around 10,000 hectares under vine that is split between around 13,000 producers. Best known for producing incredibly pricey Cabernet Sauvignon-based blends from its somewhat long and complicated classification system of 1855, Bordeaux can be broken down into sub-regions or communes, of which there are thirty-seven in total. These are determined by the river Gironde and its estuaries.

Bordeaux's weapon of choice is Cabernet Sauvignon, although there is more Merlot planted than any other variety. There are also plantings of Cabernet Franc, Malbec, and Petit Verdot, while the main white varieties are Sémillon and Sauvignon Blanc. These are primarily used to make dry white table wines, but perhaps more importantly, they produce the famous sweet wines of Sauternes and Barsac.

France is the Holy Grail of wine – the original soul brother

Burgundy. Trek to the other side of France and you'll find Burgundy – the international mecca of the wine-lover! At best, Burgundy produces some of the most seductive and interesting wines found anywhere in the world. This region, the spiritual home of Pinot Noir and Chardonnay, is located east of Paris and extends from the Chablis district in the north, to Beaujolais in the south.

Burgundy is one of the more complicated, and at times frustrating, regions for consumers to get their heads around. Like Bordeaux, it has a classification system where vineyards are graded depending on their quality: *grand cru*; *premier cru*; *village,* or the basic (and affordable) *vin du pays.* However, unlike Bordeaux and much of the rest of the winemaking world,

the vineyards of Burgundy (in all but a few cases) are often split up among a multitude of different growers rather than being individually owned. This can lead to problems in that no matter how good the reputation of the vineyard, the reputations of individual producers vary greatly, and two wines from the same vineyard made by two different people will never ever be the same.

It's super important that when buying wine from this part of the world, you know, or know someone who knows, the good producers from the bad. A Matt Skinner motto to know goes something like this: the reputation of the producer counts for everything, and never is that more true than in Burgundy!

The Rhône Valley, located directly below Burgundy's most southerly point, is sliced across the middle to form two major wine-producing areas – northern Rhône and southern Rhône. Being further south, the Rhône enjoys a much warmer climate than Burgundy, and, as a result, sees a number of different varieties popping up.

The Northern Rhône rock star red variety is Syrah (a.k.a. Shiraz, *see* p.79). It produces the flagship wines of Hermitage, Crozes-Hermitage, Cornas, and the much famed Côte-Rôtie, where Syrah is often crushed and fermented with a small percentage of native white grape variety, Viognier, to make some of the most incredibly aromatic red wines found anywhere – think super-dooper dark-berried fruit meet aromas and flavours of apricot and black pepper. Just awesome!

With around thirteen red varieties planted, alongside two native whites (Marsanne and Roussanne), understanding the wines of the southern Rhône is somewhat less simple! But the three most important varieties are Grenache, Syrah, and Mourvèdre, which appear in many combinations dominating the red blends in the area. The most important sub-regions are St Joseph, Côtes du Rhône, Gigondas, and the much-famed Châteauneuf-du-Pape.

Burgundy – the international mecca of the wine-lover

6pm | British Airways the tasting panel | the tasters

at 30,000 feet, wine tastes different!

Peter Nixson and his "Dream Team" taste hundreds
of samples to keep their passengers happy in the air!

Alsace sits in the top right-hand corner of France. Home to Hansel and Gretel-like villages, it has been caught in the crossfire during a number of conflicts between France and Germany. It is a fiercely independent region, with winemakers who produce some of the greatest and unbelievably long-lived examples of Riesling, Gewürztraminer, and Pinot Gris. The wines are richer in style than those of Germany, and tend to be fermented to complete or near dryness.

Champagne is just south of Alsace. This is without doubt one of the best examples of luxury goods marketing in the world. I mean think about it, basically we're talking about well-constructed table wine – only fizzy, super expensive, and made with unripe grapes! Sound appealing? I didn't think so... That said, the process of Champagne blending (an annual occurrence) is an art that has taken many hundreds of years to perfect. Located about two hours' drive northeast of Paris, the towns of Reims and Epernay make up the soul and pulse of the Champagne region. The native varieties are Chardonnay, Pinot Noir, and Pinot Meunier.

germany

Understanding German wine can be like trying to learn algebra – not easy (well, at least if you slept through most of the lessons, like me). Thankfully, drinking – and more importantly – enjoying some of the greatest white wines on earth doesn't require the same Buddhist-like concentration.

Yes, Germany is responsible for some of the most amazingly pure examples of Riesling produced anywhere in this, or any, galaxy (no matter how far away). The best ones, and we're talking about utterly awesome stuff here, are wines that run with all the precision of a finely-tuned Mercedes; wines that will long outlive any of us; wines that are so so great with a broad range of food styles; wines that, on the whole, represent truly outstanding value for money..., but then why are they so hard to understand?

For many years, a complex system of labelling has been the main problem. Together with having to know who the good producers are, consumers are expected to understand vineyard names and various terms indicating sweetness and vintage variation. It's exhausting just thinking about it! The following list is a basic introduction to German labelling. I hope it helps!

enjoying some of the greatest white wines on earth
doesn't require Buddhist-like concentration

- QbA (Qualitätswein bestimmter Anbaugebiete): big thumbs up! Means good-quality wine from a good-quality region.
- QmP (Qualitätswein mit Prädikat): double thumbs up, even better than QbA! And within this category comes the following:

Kabinett Not a cupboard, but a spankingly dry and usually pretty light, delicate wine.

Spätlese These are late-picked grapes, so the wines should have more weight and richness than Kabinett. Also released a few months later than Kabinett.

Auslese Get your sweet tooth out! Usually made from selected bunches of even later harvested grapes that are bursting with flavour and, in some cases, beginning to rot.

Beerenauslese OK, all this sugar is beginning to make my left leg shake. Nothing to do with beer, these wines are made from individually picked, late-harvested berries that are made up of about 19 degrees of sugar!

Trockenbeerenauslese (TBA) So sweet that my teeth have just dissolved! TBA is only made in exceptional years and requires individually selected berries – each one having around 25 degrees of sugar, with super high acidity. Usually made in seriously small quantities due to huge rarity factor.

Eiswein Similar to TBA, but grapes are picked as frozen berries and lightly pressed to give super-sweet juice.

The next class is a brief summary of the most important German regions:

The Mosel has to be seen to believed. As the river Mosel winds its way from Trier in the south toward its junction with the Rhine at Koblenz in the north, the near vertical slopes of the Mosel landscape provide a dramatic backdrop for some of Germany's greatest vineyards. How local growers work these slopes is just mind-boggling. This region – largely planted out to Riesling – produces wines of awesome intensity, delicacy, spice, and floral lift.

The Rheingau is found east of the Mosel and is located on the slopes of the river Rhine. It is also largely planted to Riesling and these give the best wines that this region has to offer. The majority of the Rheingau benefits from south-facing slopes and unusually long periods of sunlight. The wines from this region tend to display a greater depth and richness than those of their Mosel neighbours, yet they still manage to demonstrate a similar finesse and grace.

The Pfalz is situated on the banks of the river Rhine heading south back towards Alsace. Sadly, this region is perhaps better known for the Müller-Thurgau grape variety that was Germany's biggest export wine as Liebfraumilch! Let's move on, shall we?

spain

Man, I love Spain. I'm mad about it – the art, the architecture, the food, and the people. Throw into the mix some great surf, a bit of flamenco (if you're feeling particularly athletic), and most importantly some killer wine and you've just about found my answer to paradise! Spain's wine scene is on the comeback trail. A revolution in vineyard practices and winemaking techniques is well under way, and it's safe to say that Spain will be home to some of Europe's hottest producers in the coming decades.

Rioja. Nowhere has the revolution within the Spanish wine industry had more of a positive impact than here. For many years, Rioja was home to some very average wines that were made in extraordinarily large volumes, and looked tired and pretty much

spent by the time they hit the market. But like many regions around the globe, what was once destined for the scrap heap is suddenly all shiny and new again! Young winemakers are rediscovering old vines, old varieties, better clones of the red grape Tempranillo, modern production techniques, and the acknowledgment that cleanliness in the winery ranks right up there with godliness. Producing close to fifteen million cases of wine per vintage, Rioja now consistently produces some of Spain's finest wines. Seven grape varieties are permitted; however, it's Tempranillo that's king of this region.

Ribera del Duero is one of the hottest wine-producing regions in Spain today. Heading west from Barcelona along the river

7pm | Ramone the sparkling winemaker | the riddler

a super-skilled job requiring a fast hand,

Ramone hand-turns up to 50,000 bottles a day at Schramsberg winery in California's Napa Valley.

8pm | Liquid Ideas the public relations team | the spin

they love their work, who wouldn't?

Some of the biggest names in wine are represented by this team – it's a tough job, but someone's got to do it.

Ebro toward Portugal, Ribera is home to some of Spain's brightest young stars. Little more than a truck stop thirty years ago, it is now Spain's fastest growing region. In fact, land is now so expensive in Ribera that industry experts reckon you just about need "gold rocks" to get anywhere near it. But behind all the shiny black Range Rovers, lie the vineyards, many of which are dominated by local variety Tinto Fino (a mutation of Tempranillo), alongside Cabernet Sauvignon and Merlot. A modern approach is taken here with many of the wines fermented in new or nearly new barriques (fancy word for barrels). As a result, wines are deeply coloured and definitely drift toward the "blockbuster" camp!

Sherry is the English corruption of the word Jerez, which is short for Jerez de la Frontera, the largest of three major cities that form the border of the sherry region in Spain's south. The best way to think of sherry is that there are four major styles produced from two varieties.

The most important variety is Palomino, accounting for three of the four styles – Fino, Amontillado, and Oloroso. Fino is the most popular, and in my opinion, one of the greatest food wines produced anywhere. The best examples are bone dry, nutty, and slightly salty with a minerally texture. The remaining variety is Pedro Ximénez (PX), which produces the fourth style that is varietally labelled and occasionally called "black sherry". Good examples are almost black in colour, incredibly viscous, and super sweet, with intense raisin and spice aromas.

portugal

When most people think Portugal, they think Mateus Rosé, but, thankfully, like perceptions of rosé, things are on the up, and a great big push is on to thrust Portugal's wine industry straight back into the hearts and minds of the modern consumer. I say "back" because chances are that if you were drinking wine thirty years ago, you'd probably have loved the odd splash of VP (Vintage Port) or Madeira after lunch. But that was then and this is now, and current market trends see drinking fortified wines (Portuguese or not) as just a fraction uncool...

The Douro. All but annihilated by phylloxera in the late 1970s, this region is an unforgiving land of rocky near-vertical vineyards whose slopes are now mainly planted with a mix of Tinta Roriz (Spain's red superstar, Tempranillo), Touriga Nacional, and Tinta Nacional. Most of the grape-growing action in the Douro Valley occurs around its stunning horizontally challenged landscape – the best wines coming from the higher vineyards where fresh acidity and good fruit make a nice change from some of the drier beasts found in other parts of the country.

Big improvements in both the vineyard and the winery have recently resulted in Douro wines that are now fresher, and most importantly, more approachable! With change sweeping the country, the Douro is leading the way. The sky is the limit and time will tell.

north america

As the oldest and most important wine-producing country outside of Europe, the USA is the fourth largest producer of wine on the planet. But global success has come at a price; it took years for the earliest US growers to realize that the reason everything they planted died wasn't just bad luck, but because their soil was full of phylloxera. And then with the problem identified and a strategy to get things back on track in place, the US government decided to go and completely outlaw alcohol! Typical...

Prohibition ran from 1913 until 1933, and even though seventy or so years on things are pretty much back on track, the lasting legacy of Prohibition still remains. It's estimated that around one-third of people in the USA only drink spirits and beer, one-third think wine is AOK, and the remaining one-third don't drink at all – not a drop!

California – the soul of the USA's wine trade, encompassing the ultra-fashionable Napa Valley, north of San Francisco, to the more southerly growing zones, such as Santa Barbara and Santa Cruz. From Disney to Dogtown, California has given us plenty, but the one area where it falls short of satisfying everyone is in its wine department. For a long time, the problem has been that wine from the really great producers is either made in such microscopic quantities that it's never seen, or simply ends up way too expensive for Joe Average (you and me!).

At the other end of the scale, and even more frightening, is the statistic that each year some Goliath-like Californian producers single-handedly churn out more wine than Australia's combined annual production. Of course, there are exceptions to the rule – good people making great wine at sensible prices – and California has its fair share of them, but be prepared to hunt them out! On a recent visit to the Napa, I was blown away by the small parcels of Syrah and Grenache that I tasted, including a handful of world-class Chardonnay and Zinfandel. Even the odd Italian variety trickles out of Sonoma County, west of the Napa.

East coast. Further north, Washington, Oregon, Idaho, and British Colombia are also proving to be great cool climate spots for a handful of whites, a few reds, and some super scarce sweet wines. The problem again is tiny production. And if you thought the east-west USA rivalry ended with gangster rap, think again! The state of New York is steadily producing some really good wines, particularly in the aromatic wine department.

9pm | Andy the cooper | the carpenter

one of the last hand-reared processes

left in winemaking, Andy Byers has made barrels for twenty years – the last twelve for Seguin Moreau in California.

10pm | Jane the wine educator | the preacher

teaching wine mus
be the best job in
the world

Jane Ferrari spreads the word to
from all walks of life for Australia

down south – south of the equator

Young, vibrant, dynamic – call it what you will – the wine-growing zone located south of the Equator brings together the countries of South America, South Africa, New Zealand, and Australia – the "New World"; the rising stars of the wine world and surely the superstars of tomorrow. A laid-back approach coupled with a global understanding and acceptance of what's going on in the rest of the world has seen the sun-drenched wines of the southern hemisphere rocket into the hearts and minds of consumers just about everywhere around the planet.

south america

In wine, South America comprises Chile and Argentina – undoubtedly two of the future superpowers of the global wine community.

Chile is a country on the up, big time! The needle-like strip of land that runs north-south the entire length of the South American continent, bordered by the Andes Mountains in the east and the Pacific Ocean in the west, Chile has been producing wine long before the USA and Australia, and just a smidge longer than South Africa.

But the real advances in Chile's wine industry have only come in the past twenty years – coinciding with the country's emergence from years of communist rule and the beginning of free trade. Chile's producers soon realized that the majority of what they were doing was pretty much second rate, and in order to compete on the world stage, things would have to change. Modern technology was embraced, international winemakers imported, and an understanding of what was going on in places like Australia and the USA was digested and implanted.

The new-look Chile quickly forged a reputation as a dependable producer of good value wines – red and white. With a climate not dissimilar to that of Australia's, varieties such as Cabernet Sauvignon, Merlot, and Chardonnay were right at home alongside others such as Sauvignon Blanc, Carmenère, and Cabernet Franc.

The current day sees Chile sitting in the hot seat, poised and ready to strike. While international investment from France and the USA increases, more and more well-travelled Chilean winemakers are taking control of the country's top wineries. Likewise, a number of better-suited varieties – and the right clones of those varieties – are finding their way into the ground. In all, Chile looks in very good shape indeed!

Chile is sitting in the hot seat, poised and ready to strike

Chile's wine areas are mazes of valleys between the Pacific Ocean and the imposingly massive Andes Mountains.

North of the capital Santiago, you'll find the Aconcagua Valley, where Cabernet Sauvignon reigns supreme, alongside varieties such as Carmenère, Syrah, and more recently, Viognier.

To the west of Santiago lies the Casablanca Valley – perhaps the coolest of Chile's wine-growing areas due to its close proximity to the sea. Cooler climate varieties such as Pinot Noir, Syrah, and Sauvignon Blanc all do well, but spring frosts can be a danger.

South of the city is the iconic Maipo Valley, where many of the big companies are based. Much of the land is planted out to a mix of international varieties, and production in the area is on a grand scale.

Finally, one the most southerly of Chile's significant wine regions is the Colchagua Valley, where a handful of Chile's new school are doing some very slick things with varieties such as Cabernet Sauvignon, Carmenère, Merlot, and Syrah.

Argentina, on the flip side of the Andes, shares similar characteristics as its neighbour, Chile – great snow, great wine, and legendary footballers. Argentina is more or less a great big desert, but it has the added bonus of unlimited water from the extremely well-situated Andes – perfect for grape-growing! And, even though Argentina, like Chile, has all the pieces to the "everything you need to make great wine" puzzle, it's fair to say that Chile is winning the race at the moment.

Increased global interest in wine has forced South America in general to lift its game. It is still early days, but the employment of both modern winemaking technology and international winemakers (dollars, too!) has brought really encouraging signs of what's to come. With a few great vintages and more

vine age, South America looks like it could be producing some world-class wines.

The majority of vineyards in Argentina are situated in regions of Mendoza and San Juan. As a rule, reds tend to do better here, with Bordeaux ex-pat, Malbec, leading the way. Interestingly, some of the highest vineyards on the planet can be found in Argentina, and are mainly planted to a mix of Malbec and Cabernet Sauvignon. The reason grapes can survive up here is due to tiny microclimates that receive maximum sun exposure and trap pockets of warmth. The altitude also arms the resulting wines with the highest level of anti-oxidants (that combat all the nasty stuff in your body) to be found anywhere. These wines are great to drink *and* seriously good for you!

australia

Australia has come a long way baby! From the giant steps taken in Australian vineyards during the early 1800s by viticultural guru James Busby, it's been little short of a slingshot ride to international stardom for Australia's wine industry. And so it continues to grow. Having won international hearts and markets alike with a reputation for producing clean – and at times clinical – fruit-driven wines, Australia has, in the last decade, proven itself as a force within the global wine community, putting Europe's major wine-producing countries on notice. But now's not the time to get complacent; there's still plenty of work to be done... The most important regions are outlined below.

South Australia is the heart and soul of Australia's wine industry. Structured around the city of Adelaide, South Oz is not only headquarters to many of Australia's major wine big guns, but, more importantly, home to some of this country's most important wine regions.

The Barossa Valley is home to some of the oldest Shiraz vines grown anywhere in the country. Back in the day when it was more fashionable to drink badly-made sherry than great, old-vine Shiraz, the South Australian government set about encouraging growers to rip out the unpopular varieties, replacing them with grapes that were. Among those on the hit list was Shiraz! Can you believe it? Those who resisted the golden carrots on offer are currently laughing all the way to the bank as owners of some of the country's (even world's) oldest Shiraz vines. Shiraz has a real affinity in the Barossa, the best vines producing inky – almost black – wines that are essays in concentration, power, and longevity.

Victoria. Consisting of a variety of vastly different regions, this is perhaps best-known as Australia's premier producer of cool climate wines. The Yarra Valley is located about forty minutes' drive east of Melbourne, and is home to Victoria's first vineyard established in 1892. Leaning toward the cooler side of grape-growing, varieties such as Pinot Noir, Chardonnay, and Shiraz all do consistently well within its boundaries.

Tasmania. In the past five years, the most southerly of Australia's grape-growing areas has come on in leaps and bounds, and is now on everyone's lips. Careful site selection and the specific use of clones – particularly with Pinot Noir – has made the Apple Isle a serious contender and perhaps even a future key New World player (with Pinot). Due to its chilly southerly exposure, Tasmania provides the best terroir for much of the country's best sparkling base wine with mainland producers sourcing fruit here for the backbone of their flagship sparkling wines. Champagne they're not, but they're definitely worthy of attention!

Western Australia. World-class surf aside, this area has, in recent times, made a significant contribution to the top end of Australia's local wine scene. In particular, Margaret River has been growing in stature for the best part of the past two decades and is home to a handful of benchmark Cabernet producers. The best of these wines combine elegance, finesse, power, and longevity.

New South Wales is the historical home of Australia's wine industry, and the Hunter Valley remains the state's most important region. What the Hunter makes really, really well is Semillon. I remember a customer who was always desperate to get his hands on these seriously old bottles (we're talking thirty odd years here!) of Hunter River Chablis (no, Chablis isn't Oz, that's what Semillon used to be called). I was always able to track a few down, but I remember thinking: why would you want to drink them? Not only were the bottles shabby to look at, but you could see that much of the wine had evaporated and had begun to turn deep-gold. They were hideously expensive, too. But still he came back for more. These bottles were like his addiction.

I couldn't understand the fuss until the day I tried one! What a revelation. Deep-gold and green to look at, but inside the glass was where the magic was. Rich aromas of citrus marmalade, toast, and spice just leapt out of the glass and smacked you around the face. Wow, it was good, and I, too, began to understand the addiction!

The fact that Australia is now enjoying a well-deserved moment in the spotlight as the fourth largest exporter of wine globally (crushing somewhere in excess of 100 million tonnes per year) can be attributed to the ongoing efforts of a group of hard-working individuals. In short, Australia's wine industry has never looked in better shape.

new zealand

We love the friendly rivalry between Australia and New Zealand! The differences in grape-growing between the two are as massive as the body of water that separates them. Australia is basically a big semi-desert; New Zealand is lush, green, and highly influenced by the bodies of water that surround it. It has developed a devoted following of wine-worshippers around the planet with its slick and skeletal style of Sauvignon Blanc, and as a country, nowhere has championed the pros of the screwcap quite like the Kiwis.

But where New Zealand competes comfortably on the world stage is in the production of other varieties such as Pinot Noir, Syrah, and Riesling. The best offerings of Pinot – the really amazing stuff – rank as some of the best examples to be found anywhere outside of Burgundy, while good Syrah and Riesling often point more than just the odd suggestive finger towards France and Germany respectively.

South island. We all know how good Marlborough Sauvignon Blanc is, hailing from the northern tip of the south island. But New Zealand also lays claim to geographically being the most southerly point you could wish to grow grapes, and it's here in Central Otago that some of the great examples of Pinot Noir and Riesling are found.

North island. Up here, world-class, insanely well-crafted examples of Pinot Noir are made in Martinborough (the southern tip of the north island) – home to the oldest Pinot plantings in the country. Halfway between Marlborough and Auckland, the slightly warmer Hawke's Bay area is home to some fine examples of Chardonnay, Syrah, and Cabernet.

a devoted following **of wine worshippers**

11pm | Philglass and Swiggot the retailers | the coalface

as local shops vanish by the minute,

**Karen and Mike Rogers made their dream come true –
they are easily London's best independent wine retailer.**

south africa

South Africa is an incredible place that, in little on ten years, has achieved mind-blowing amounts. When apartheid ended in 1994, South Africa was once again free to trade with the rest of the world. They were in for a rude awakening. A genuine lack of resources combined with an inability to accept that they were not in fact producing "the greatest wines on the face of the earth" meant that there was plenty to be done and no time to waste. Ten years on, and South Africa's wine industry is a very different place. As the fourth largest supplier of wine by value to the UK, South Africa is once again a force to be reckoned with.

Grapes and determination. Highlighting where the advances have been made is harder than it might sound, although picking out the best spots to plant vines; choosing the right grape varieties; and a massive determination to create wines that aren't all about big fruit, but, more importantly, about structure and finesse, have all played a significant role.

But wait, there's more! By far the most exciting thing happening in South Africa's wine scene currently is the rise and development of Black Economic Empowerment projects, the goals of which are to help previously disadvantaged South Africans build a better future.

The next generation of South African winemakers are chomping at the bit to start making awesome wines. They have studied, some from empowerment projects, graduated, travelled, and firmly understood the importance of preserving the Cape's winemaking heritage, but they are also moving their industry forward.

Never before has there been such a variety of styles at such a level of quality. However, there is still much to be done, and the winemakers of the Cape, new and old, know this better than anyone.

Stellenbosch and Paarl. South Africa's wine industry is centred around Stellenbosch (home of the legendary Acker pub!). Outside of Stellenbosch, world-class examples of Cabernet Sauvignon, Cabernet Franc, Chardonnay, and Sauvignon Blanc are coming from the surrounding areas of Elsenburg, Paarl, Helderberg, and the Elgin Valley. East of Stellenbosch, the region of Franschhoek is kicking some major goals.

Franschhoek is arguably the culinary capital of the Cape with some awesome restaurants, world-class chefs, and a ton of great local produce. The wine scene in Franschhoek is similarly tidy with a handful of small- to medium-sized producers doing incredible things with varieties such as Syrah, Sémillon, and Cabernet Sauvignon. I am certain that there will be plenty more to hear about this area in the next few years.

the best of the rest

One of the best things about my job is the constant reminder that wine is produced in some unexpected and faraway places!

India. I'll never forget the day that I first tried Indian wine – I thought someone was playing a joke on me! Better still, I was really happy to find that it was good – so good, in fact, that it even had me thinking it was from somewhere in southern France! While I'm holding myself back from shouting the virtues of Indian wine to the heavens, there is little doubt that India could make very good wine in years to come.

China. Yeah, you heard right, China – destined to be one of the serious wine superpowers of the future. Chinese grape-growers have, for a number of years, been labouring away in the vineyards surrounding Beijing. Riesling and Chardonnay are the two varieties that really stand out. There are others, including a handful of red varieties, such as Cabernet and Merlot. But, on the whole, it's whites that tend to do better in China's wild and wacky maritime climate. Right now, the price of many of the wines is a real issue, but things will no doubt sort themselves out over time. Fingers crossed!

Greece. Back to more familiar territory. A combination of screwcaps, posh new wineries, great international press, even the first Greek Master of Wine, have all been the result of a very deliberate twenty-year Herculean push to haul Greece's wine industry into modern times. Not only did the Greeks invent the Olympics, but, 6,000 years

earlier, there is some evidence to suggest that they invented wine, too! You'll find all the usual suspects here: Cabernet, Syrah, Chardonnay, and Viognier are right at home, alongside local varieties such as Assyrtiko, Malagousia, and Agiorgitiko. And, with a rash of suitable growing areas dotted around the country, the picture-perfect island of Santorini, with its combination of low rainfall, little irrigation, and plenty of volcanic ash, ensures Greece's very best offerings – mainly dry summery whites. Check them out.

And then there's good old English wine...

England. Trust me, this isn't a matter of sour grapes (boom boom!), but England just shouldn't be good at producing wine. In fact, the evidence against it is compelling.

At the end of the day, a complex equation of the wrong varieties, poor geographical location (England is about as far north of the Equator as you could ever grow grapes), constant rainfall, lack of hills, not much sun, and overly fertile soil all conspire to work against the UK in its bid to grow grapes. So, you can imagine my surprise when I was recommended English sparkling wine!

What makes these producers really special is hard to pin down, but there's no doubt that a fifteen-million-year-old vein of chalk linking Champagne and West Sussex, quite a few US dollars, and some smooth French winemaking skills have all certainly helped. The result is some stonkingly good wines, a string of great show results, and more than just the odd, confused, red-faced wine critic.

thirsty words

Talk about taking the fun out of it! Wine is an awesome subject that is often perceived as being more than just a wee bit tricky due to the language that it lugs around. Sadly, for most of us, the idea of having to learn a whole new vocabulary is a case of too much hard work and not enough time. Listed alphabetically, the following is a collection of the twenty-one most misunderstood, confusing, mind-bending, and just downright weird words that are commonly used (or misused) in the great big world of wine!

1. Acid. If Jimi Hendrix was still here, I'm sure he'd have a very different explanation to mine on this one, but just so you know, wine contains a number of different types of acid, and apart from being a natural preservative, it's what makes wine taste crisp and refreshing. The most common type of acid found in wine is tartaric and malic, both of which you should notice in fizz and whites more easily than you will reds.

2. Balance. Remember school assembly when you used to have to sing and there was always one teacher who was out of time, out of tune, and much, much louder than everyone else? Well, this is a good example of something that's "out of balance". Wine is a sum of its parts – fruit, oak, acid, and tannin mainly, and when assembled, these things should all work together harmoniously with no one thing – like an off-key teacher – dominating!

3. Bouquet. No, there's not a great big bunch of flowers in every glass! In fact, the word bouquet in the wine world, like aroma, simply refers to the range of things that you can smell in a wine – mainly fruit and oak aromas.

4. Botrytis (*bot-rite-iss*). This is a type of airborne fungus that attacks grapes, sucks out all the water, concentrates the grape's sugar, and then leaves them to rot! Sounds nasty, I know, but a lot of winemakers encourage botrytis in certain white varieties, as the resulting rotten grapes (which aren't bad for you) produce some of the planet's greatest sweet wines.

5. Brettanomyces (*bret-ano-my-sees*). Undoubtedly the buzz wine word of the moment, Brettanomyces, or "Brett" as the true pro likes to call it, is a type of yeast spoilage that lives and breeds in wine barrels. Most commonly, Brett finds itd way into finished wine, imparting an unmistakable smell of sterile plastic, and in particular, band-aids.

6. Clones. Admittedly the term clone sounds a bit "Close Encounters-ish", but a clone in the wine world is simply a sub-variety or mutated strain of a particular grape. The emergence of new varieties occurs in much the same way a family tree develops and splinters over time. Vine cuttings are transported from one place to another, where, subjected to a different set of climatic conditions, different soils, even different kinds of diseases, they'll be forced to mutate and change.

7. Corked. The term "corked" is used to describe a wine fault caused by bacteria known as TCA. All corks begin life as tree bark, and somewhere between here and getting rammed into a wine bottle, around seven per cent of corks end up becoming affected. You can't tell a wine is corked by looking at it – it's not mould on the top of your cork and it's not crumbly cork in your wine – you can only smell and/or taste it. At worst, it smells like wet cardboard, and it strips the wine of all its beautiful fruit. If you're in doubt, take or send it back and it should be happily replaced for you!

8. Dumb. If you ever hear an "in-the-know" taster refer to a wine as being "a bit dumb", relax; they're not sinking the boots into the wine and calling it stupid. The term really just refers to a wine that isn't giving much in the way of aroma or flavour. Some varieties, Riesling in particular, go through a "dumb phase" shortly after being bottled while they adjust to being in a confined space. Given a bit of time, they come good again.

9. Funky. Yep, believe it or not, wine can be funky! Not in a James Brown style, though. Funky is a tasting term often used to describe a wine that has a kind of earthy/animal edge to it. It's not necessarily seen as a negative character, although too much "funk" can throw a wine out of balance. What would the Godfather have to say about that I wonder?

10. Grog. A great – no, the greatest – and most underrated Australian term for alcohol, and in particular wine! The term allegedly goes back a couple of hundred years to when a grogram cloak-wearing Admiral ordered the watering down of rum. Understandably, his troops weren't all that happy with him, and, as a result, dubbed their new lighter rum "grog". Can be used like this: "Have we got any grog left?"

thirsty words cont.

11. Legs. Some wines will cling to the glass when you give them a good old swirl, while others will appear thinner and less viscous – this is known as the wine's "legs". The most important thing to remember is that whether or not you can see wine hanging onto the side of a glass, it doesn't have any bearing whatsoever on the overall quality of the wine.

12. Lees (*leez*). OK, remember back to when we were talking about fermentation? Yeast is added to grape juice, where it shoots around "Pac-Man style" munching up the sugar and converting it to alcohol, the result being wine. But once Pac-Man has done his job, he dies and slowly floats to the bottom of the tank or barrel. This dead yeast is known as "lees", and its job doesn't stop there! Rather than removing it, some winemakers like to leave it in or even give it a good old stir – particularly in Chardonnay – which ends up giving the wine some good nutty, creamy flavours.

13. Magnum. Contrary to popular opinion, a "magnum" in wine circles is neither Dirty Harry's weapon of choice, nor is it a Ferrari-driving private detective from Hawaii! A magnum is, however, a large format wine bottle that holds 1,500ml or the same amount as two standard wine bottles. Magnums – more a novelty than anything else – are useful for serious collectors, as they age at a much slower rate than a standard 750ml bottle due to a greater wine-to-oxygen ratio.

14. Malolactic fermentation (MLF). This is the process whereby malic acid (think tart Granny Smith apples) is transferred into lactic acid (think milk). This process occurs naturally in all red wines, but has to be kick-started in whites, where it is really only employed in varieties such as Chardonnay and Sémillon, softening excessively high acidity and producing smells of butterscotch and cream.

15. Minerally. Ok, I know I use this word a lot, but, to me, "minerally" means a few things. Aromatically, a wine can smell minerally in much the same way that water can when it is full of things like magnesium and potassium. I also use minerally to describe a wine's texture – like when you take a mouthful of fresh water from a stream and it's really fresh, light, and delicate. For example, Riesling can be minerally, Pinot Grigio can be minerally, but rarely – if ever – is Viognier minerally!

16. Oily. Different to a big greasy bag of chips, "oily" refers to a kind of texture that a wine has in your mouth. Certain varieties and some wines that are higher in alcohol leave a natural slippery feeling in your mouth.

17. Punt. This is the indentation in the bottom of a bottle, particularly prominent in Champagne and sparkling wine bottles, and is designed to strengthen the glass against internal pressure.

18. Tannin. Apart from the obvious, which is colour, the main difference between white wine and red wine is that reds contain tannin. Tannin, also found in tea, is a type of acid that comes from grape skins, grape pips, and wood. You can't smell or taste tannin, but it's that really dry feeling that you get at the back of your mouth after a big swig of red wine.

19. Terrior (*te-wah*). French word "terrior" is tricky as it doesn't really have a straightforward English translation. In a nutshell, terrior is more of a concept that ultimately defines the identity of a place – or in the case of wine, a plot of land. Sun, soil, sea, wind, rain, plants, animals, people, my football team (well, maybe not my football team), the universe, the galaxy – all of these and more, much much more, will have a massive impact on how a particular wine from a particular place will end up tasting. It's regionalism on steroids. *Comprenez-vous?* This is terrior.

20. Phylloxera (*fill-ox-er-a*). Nasty stuff. Most commonly spread by foot (*i.e.* the tourist), phylloxera is a root-eating louse that destroys whole vines by munching away at their root system until they subsequently fall over and die. Not good.

21. Woody. Settle down boys, the term "woody" is used to describe the smell of oak in a wine. A combination of fire and water are used to bend oak staves in the production of oak barrels. Winemakers can request the level of "toasting" or how long the barrel spends over the fire once it's assembled, depending on how much influence, or "woody flavour", they want in the final wine!

index

12am **cheers**

First and foremost a massive thanks has to go to my wife and best friend, Carls – without your love, encouragement, and support, none of this would have ever happened. Thank you beautiful, for everything x.

To my Mum for a lifetime of sacrifices and for always being there for me.

To the rest of the clan, Drew, Caroline, Anne, and Eric the dog for all the good times.

To my friend and mentor Philip Rich for taking me under your wing many moons ago!

CT – world's best photographer and my Thirsty Work co-pilot! Here's to non-stop laughs, excess baggage, and the worst seats on the plane every time! Thanks for being such a diamond mate, and here's to our next Thirsty adventure!

Jay – for every door opened, every bit of good advice, friendship, loyalty, and support. Thank you always.

To David Gleave and Stuart Gregor for extreme generosity and all the amazing opportunities.

To Paul Green and Josh Clark, my right-hand men, who without, I'd be lost!

Hils, Yash, Jane, and all at Mitchell Beazley – thanks for such a painless ride guys! It's been brilliant working with you so far.

To Sophie Waggett, Dalene Steyn, and Wines of South Africa, Michael Cox, Pilar Valverde and Wines of Chile, Andrew Tierney (Wirra Wirra), Matt Thompson, and Joe Cafaro for making the Thirsty Work World Tour awesome!

Love, support, inspiration, and endless good times in no particular order from Jimmy and Caela, Simon and Hayley, Lisa Sullivan and Fresh Partners, Sweet as Candy, Matt Utber and Imperfectionist, Lindsey Evans, Randy, Tobes, and Gyros, Thommo, Gin and Camilla, CC and BP, the Jones and Duncan clans, Liquid Ideas, John and Frank van Haandel, Paula Dupuy and Fifteen, Fifteen trainees – past and present, the Whitehorse Inn, the late Mark Shield, The Juice, VB, The Hawks, and all at the crew back home in Melbourne...

Stay Thirsty, M x